COL

COLONSAY
One of the Hebrides

Its Plants: Their Local Names and Uses
Legends, Ruins and Place Names
Gaelic Names of Birds, Animals and Fishes
Notes on Climate and Geology

by Murdoch McNeill

First published 1910, David Douglas, Edinburgh
This edition 2001, House of Lochar

ISBN 1 899863 36 2

Cover illustration by Lucy McNeill

Printed in Great Britain by SRP, Exeter
for House of Lochar, Isle of Colonsay, Argyll PA61 7YR

PREFACE TO FIRST EDITION

A COLLECTION of the plants of his native island was begun
by the writer in 1903, during a period of convalescence, and
was continued as a recreation, from time to time, as occasion
offered. In 1908 the idea of making use of the material
accumulated and arranging it for publication was conceived,
and to put it into effect a final endeavour was made that
season to have the plant list of the island as complete as the
circumstances would permit.

In preparing the little volume for the press, the lack of
works of reference was found a serious drawback. The
following publications were found most helpful :— Bentham
and Hooker's *British Flora* ; Withering's *English Botany* ;
Cameron's *Gaelic Names of Plants* ; Hogan's *Irish and
Scottish Gaelic Names of Herbs, Plants, Trees, etc.* ; Gregory's
History of the West Highlands ; *Oransay and its Monastery*,
by F. C. E. M'Neill; "Colla Ciotach Mac Ghilleasbuig," by
Prof. Mackinnon (*Celtic Monthly*, Sept. 1903–Jan. 1904) ;
Geikie's *Scenery of Scotland* ; *Notes on the Geology of Colon-
say and Oransay*, by Prof. Geikie; *The Two Earth-Movements
of Colonsay*, by W. B. Wright, B.A., F.G.S. ; *Sketch of the
Geology of the Inner Hebrides*, by Prof. Heddle ; Journals of

the Scottish Meteorological Society; Address on the Climate of the British Isles, by A. Watt, M.A., etc.

Among the many friends who have given generous aid, special thanks are due to two gentlemen in particular: Mr Arthur Bennett, F.L.S., who has named or verified nearly all the Colonsay plants; and Professor Mackinnon, of the Celtic Chair, Edinburgh, a native of Colonsay, who kindly read the proof-sheets and corrected the Gaelic names. Others kindly gave help in a variety of ways. Thus Mr E. B. Bailey, who was engaged for several seasons in the Geological Survey of the island, corrected and amplified the chapter on Geology.

In determining doubtful species, assistance was received from the authorities at Kew and the following gentlemen :— Rev. W. Moyle Rogers, F.L.S., Bournemouth (Rubi); Mr W. Barclay, Perth (Rosa); Rev. E. S. Marshall, M.A., F.L.S., Taunton (Euphrasia, Betula, etc.); Rev. E. F. Linton, M.A., Salisbury (Mentha, Hieracia, Salix, etc.); Mr Charles T. Druery, F.L.S., Acton (Ferns); the late Rev. W. R. Linton, M.A. (Hieracia); Rev. G. R. Bullock Webster, F.L.S. (Chara, Tolypella).

For information concerning the plants of the surrounding islands and assistance in other ways, the writer is much indebted to Mr Symers M. MacVicar (flora of Tiree, Eigg, Lismore, etc.), Dr Gilmour (list of the Islay plants), Mr P. Ewing, F.L.S. (Glasgow Catalogue of Native and Established Plants), Dr M'Neill, Medical Officer of the County of Argyll, and others; and to Mr Donald M'Neill, Lower Kilchattan, and the older inhabitants for information on local matters.

The writer trusts that much of the matter contained in the following pages may be regarded as typical of and applicable in many respects to the Western Islands as a whole. He would gladly have entered into greater detail regarding the old-time industries, place-names, topography, traditions, and folk-lore of Colonsay, but the general reader may be of opinion that enough has been said on these matters in a work primarily intended to treat of the flora of the island.

M. M^{C}N.

KILORAN, COLONSAY,
  December 1909.

The first edition was dedicated to
the first Lord Strathcona, thus:

THIS VOLUME IS

Respectfully Dedicated

TO THE RIGHT HONOURABLE

LORD STRATHCONA AND MOUNT ROYAL,

G.C.M.G., G.C.V.O., D.C.L., LL.D., D.L.

IN ACKNOWLEDGMENT OF HIS GENEROUS ASSISTANCE,

WHICH HAS ENABLED THIS VOLUME TO BE

COMPLETED AND PUBLISHED

CONTENTS

COLONSAY

ONE OF THE HEBRIDES

CHAPTER I

GENERAL DESCRIPTION

THE islands of Colonsay and Oransay and the neighbouring
islands of Islay, Jura, and Scarba, with their islets, constitute
the group of the South Inner Hebrides. Colonsay and
Oransay were formerly jointly known as Eilean Tarsuinn
(or the cross-lying island), so designated, it would seem,
from an exaggerated notion of their oblique position with
relation to the Sound of Islay. In the *Old Statistical
Account* it is mentioned, but erroneously, that they are
named after two saints, Colon and Oran.

Colonsay (Gaelic, *Colasa*) is 9 miles long, and averages 3
in breadth ; with Oransay, the length is 12 miles. Situated
in lat. 56° 5′ N., long. 6° 15′ W., the island is distant by sea
from Greenock about 110 miles and from Oban about 38.
In striking contrast to the opposite island of Jura, whose
Paps rise steeply from the Atlantic to a height of 2571 feet,
and the more distant Mull, where Ben Mor attains an
altitude of 3169 feet, Colonsay is low-lying ; Carnan Eoin,
its highest hill, not exceeding 470 feet above sea-level.
The channel that separates it from the nearest islands
varies in breadth from 8 to 20 miles, widening from south

to north. The depth of the channel generally is less than 20 fathoms, but north of the island the sea deepens considerably with an irregular bottom.

Notwithstanding the low elevation, in clear weather distant views of the other islands and of the mainland can be obtained. Northward, beyond the isles of Iona, Tiree, and Coll, the outline of what is thought to be the peak of Ben Heavel (1260 feet) in Barra, 70 miles away, has been observed. The hills of Donegal in Ireland to the south-west, and Goatfell in Arran, 44 miles off, are more frequently seen. In winter the snow-capped Ben Cruachan and other Argyllshire hills, and even Ben Nevis, 60 miles distant, are familiar objects on the horizon in the north-east. On the western side the wide sweep of the Atlantic is broken only by the lonely Du Hirteach lighthouse (15 miles off) and a few barren rocks; the Skerryvore light flashing into view across the intervening 37 miles of sea only when the sky is very clear.

For several hours during low water the smaller island of Oransay is connected with the southern end of Colonsay by a sandy, islet-dotted strand. Oransay (Gaelic, *Orasa*) is derived from the Norse (*Orjiris-ey* = ebb-tide island). The name is common in the West, there being some twenty of them between the western shores and islands. Oransay is about 2000 acres in extent, and hilly on the north; its highest hill, Beinn Orasa, being 308 feet above sea-level. The southern portion is low-lying, with sand-dunes overgrown with Sea Maram, Sea Sedge, and other plants and mosses, which assist in binding the sand. With the exception of some shrubby Willows and Elders, the island is treeless.

After his departure from Ireland in 563, St Columba is said to have landed at Oransay, but there is no historical record confirming this tradition. Port-na-h-Iùbhraich (Port of the Barge), at Iochdar-na-Garbhaird, on the west side of the Strand, has been suggested as his probable landing-place. According to local tradition, this was also the spot where, at a later date, the galley of a viking chief came ashore. It is related of St Columba that before he left Ireland he made a vow never to settle within sight of his native hills, and discovering that he could still see them from the Beinn in Oransay, he moved to Iona.

The earliest mention that we have of Colonsay is in Adamnan's Life of St Columba, which was written about A.D. 693, *i.e.* about ninety-six years after the saint's death. The name in Adamnan's Latin is Colosus. In this, the oldest book which can be proved to have been written in Scotland, the author relates an interesting story of one Erc Mocudruidi, who had the hardihood to cross, in a small boat, the stormy strip of ocean that separates Colonsay from Iona, with the intention of stealing the seals that St Columba was rearing for his own use. He hid his coracle among the sand-hills in Mull, on the opposite side of the sound, and, in concealment, waited for the fall of night for carrying out his dishonest design. St Columba, perceiving his purpose, sent two of the brethren to apprehend him. "Why dost thou often steal the goods of others, transgressing the divine command? When thou art in need, come, and then thou shalt receive for the asking all that is necessary," said the saint when the culprit was brought before him; and, lest he should return empty, he caused sheep to be killed for him. Foreseeing in spirit that the death of the thief was at hand, St Columba ordered Baithene in Tiree to send to him to Colonsay, as a last gift, a fat sheep and six pecks of corn. On the day that the presents arrived Mocudruidi died suddenly, and the gifts were used by the mourners at the funeral feast.

The Norwegians held the Western Islands for upwards of 400 years, and although it is nearly 650 years since they lost possession, evidences of their occupation are not wanting in

Colonsay in place-names—*e.g.* Poll-na-Cnarradh (Ga. *Poll* =
pool, Nor. *Knarr* = vessel; *i.e.* the Pool of the Vessel),
Scalasaig (Bay of Small Huts), Cnoc Innibrig (Knoll of
Ingibiorg), etc.—in legends, and in interments such as were
dug up at Lag-na-Birlinn, Machrins golf-links, and at Traigh-
nam-Bàrc. Bronze coins of Wigmund, Archbishop of York
A.D. 837–854, similar to one recently found in a ship-burial
in the island of Arran, were discovered in the viking's grave
at Lag-na-Birlinn. A sword, rusty and almost mouldered
away, was lying near the bones of the warrior who met
his death at Traigh-nam-Bàrc, the local tradition in connection with it being, that a fight took place in the vicinity
between natives and the Norsemen who landed from the
galley at Port-na-h-Iùbhraich. The leader of the latter was
killed, and his body encased in the stone coffin, which lay in
the ground undisturbed for more than 600 years. Three
of the principal hill-forts—Dun Eibhinn, Dun Ghallain,
and Dun Cholla—are said to have been named after
three sons—Edmund, Gallan, and Coll—of the King of
Lochlann. In one of the Norse sagas mention is made
of a certain Earl Gilli, Lord of Coln (Colonsay or Coll?),
being married in the eleventh century to a Norwegian lady
of high rank.

The Druid's circle, some rough stones arranged in a
circular manner at Buaile Riabhach, recalls a still more
remote and mysterious past. Britain, before the Roman
invasion, was the stronghold of Druidism, and not until the
Celtic people were converted to Christianity did this form of
worship entirely disappear from their midst. The *cill 's* are
of Christian origin. They are the remains of chapels which
were in use before, some of them after, the Reformation.
Sites of about a dozen of these old structures are pointed out
in various places in the island. Portions of the walls of two
—Temple of the Glen and Kilchattan—are yet standing,
and, judging by what is still seen of the walls, they were of

small size. Gravestones show that burials were made within
and around the buildings. Of some of these old structures
hardly a trace now remains. Time, in its work of destruc-
tion, was aided by man, who found the stones (as well
as those constructing the duns) useful for various other
purposes. The dedications were to Columba (Oransay),
Oran, Catan, Ciaran, Coinneach, Maol - Rubha (Cill-á-
Rubha), Moire (Mary—two dedications, one in Colonsay
and one in Oransay), Brìde (Bridget), and Catrìona
(Catherine).

Among the possessions confirmed by David II. in 1344 to
John, Lord of the Isles, we find Colonsay included. The
island was occupied until the seventeenth century by the
M'Duffies or M'Phees. They held it from the M'Donalds, but
there is no evidence to show at what period they first came
into possession, or indeed that they ever had a written charter
of the island. After the forfeiture of the Lordship of the
Isles, M'Phee, like M'Donald of Islay, became a tenant of
the Crown. M'Phee was clerk or secretary to the council
or parliament of the M'Donalds of Islay. Their stronghold
was evidently Dun Eibhinn, from which their title of Lord
of Dun Eibhinn, engraved on a tombstone in Iona, had been
derived. A Donald M'Duffie or M'Phee of Colonsay witnessed a charter of John, Earl of Ross, in 1463. In 1609
another of the name and designation was present at the
assembly of island chiefs in Iona presided over by Bishop
Knox, when the nine famous statutes of Icolmkill were
enacted.

Something of the history of the M'Phees may be learned
from the inscriptions on their tombstones. Their burial-
place was a small chapel built against the south wall of the
church in Oransay. It contained some of the sculptured
stones now arranged along the north side of the church.
One of these is to the memory of Murchardus M'Duffie,
who died in 1539. Another was over the tomb of Sir

Donald M'Duffie, abbot in Oransay when Dean Monro made his tour of the Western Isles in 1549. Monro wrote that "the Ile is brucket by ane gentle capitane callit M'Duffybe, and pertained of auld to clan Donald of Kintyre."

The last of the M'Phees of Colonsay, Malcolm M'Phee, was killed at Eilean-nan-Ròn, south of Oransay, by Coll Ciotach in February 1623. Earlier in the century he, according to Gregory, had been compelled for a time to hold his lands from Argyll, instead of M'Donald of Islay. This circumstance, however, did not prevent him from joining Sir James M'Donald when the latter escaped from Edinburgh Castle in 1615. The rising was unsuccessful, and at its close M'Phee was delivered into the hands of Argyll by Coll Ciotach, one of his associates in the recent revolt.

After being detained for some time as a prisoner in Edinburgh, M'Phee was allowed to return to Colonsay. Places of concealment in various parts of the island, named after him (leab' fhalaich Mhic-a-Phì), indicate that he had been hunted about from place to place for some time before his death. He was finally followed to the south-western extremity of Eilean-nan-Ròn, an-t-Eilean-Iarach, but would have still remained undiscovered had not his whereabouts been made known to his pursuers in a curious manner. Coll and his men were returning to Oransay after a fruitless search when the cry of a gull hovering over a particular spot attracted their attention, and on reaching the place they found M'Phee crouching on a very narrow ledge of rock at the edge of the sea. "Fàbhar, a Thàmhais," pleaded the fugitive. "Fàbhar no fàbhar," answered Tàmhas Mac 'Ille Mhoirche, the person who first saw him, "is beag fàbhair a gheibhteadh o t' fheusaig ruaidh mu'n àm so 'n dé." In June 1623 Coll and his son Gilleasbuig, with four followers, were summoned to Edinburgh on the charge of murdering Malcolm M'Phee of Colonsay, Donald (Og) M'Phee, Dugald

M'Phee, John M'Quarrie, and Ivor Bàn (the Fair), the complainants being Mary M'Donald (M'Phee's widow), Donald, a son, Catherine, Annie, and Flora, daughters, besides relatives of the other victims.

Although the history of the island is often veiled in obscurity, we can gather from various sources that its ownership during the latter half of the sixteenth century and the early part of the seventeenth was a source of contention among the M'Phees, M'Donalds, M'Leans, and Campbells. After the forfeiture of the Lordship of the Isles in 1493, the Isles, instead of following one leader, were divided among a number of chiefs who frequently opposed one another. In their quarrels over the ownership of certain parts of Islay, M'Lean of Duart and M'Donald of Islay were fighting for close on half a century, 1550–1600. Local traditions of raids and clan fights are often associated with this period.

The battle of Traigh Ghruineart in the north of Islay, in 1598, brought the long tribal warfare between the M'Leans and M'Donalds to a close. Before the fight began, Dubh-sìth Beag, a native of Jura, asked Lachlan Mòr, chief of the M'Leans, for "a day's work." Owing to his diminutive size, M'Lean refused to take him into his ranks. Nothing daunted, Dubh-sìth went to the opposite party. M'Donald gave him "a man's place." "I will see to Lachlan Mòr; you dispose of the rest," exclaimed the dwarf, who forthwith betook himself to the shelter of some neighbouring scrub. In the heat of the fight, Lachlan Mòr bent down to arrange his armour. Dubh-sith, who was an expert bowman, seeing part of M'Lean's person unprotected by his coat of mail while he was in this position, shot him with an arrow. Besides their chief, nearly 300 of the M'Leans fell on that day. The M'Donalds' loss was not so great, but their chief, Sir James M'Donald, Lachlan Mor's nephew, was wounded.

The person whose doings during this stormy period most

vividly impressed the imagination of succeeding generations of islanders was Colla Ciotach (Mac Gilleasbuig) M'Donald. Although we do not know the date of his arrival in Colonsay, he was long connected with the island. According to local tradition, he came from Ireland. The date of his birth was about 1570. His grandfather, Coll, was brother to James M'Donald of Dun Naomhaig, and of the Glens in Ireland, the first Earl of Antrim being a cousin. It is said that Coll was twice married, and local tradition hands down an incident in connection with the burial of one of his wives. M'Donald of Keppoch had been married to a woman much younger than himself. For a slighting retort which she made when he was in a playful mood, " Se sin miolaran an t-seana choin ris a chuilein," he sent her away, and she afterwards lived with Coll in Colonsay as his wife. M'Donald, later on, found his way to the island. Coll, on hearing of his arrival, went to apprise his wife, who had been but recently confined. Wishing to find out if she still had any regard for her former husband, he told her that M'Donald had been drowned off the Point of Ardnamurchan. On hearing this, she turned away her face and expired. A dispute subsequently arose between Coll and Keppoch as to where the body should be taken for burial, Kilchattan or Oransay; and to settle the matter they resorted to a duel of spears at the western entrance of the mansion-house, afterwards known as Bealach an t-Sleagh (Gateway of the Spear).

Two of Coll Ciotach's sons, Alastair and Angus, are referred to in local tradition; but not the third, Gilleasbuig. Alastair, Montrose's celebrated general, was born in the Abbey barn (Sabhall Bàn), Kiloran, used as the family residence after the old Abbey had fallen into a dilapidated condition. It was an indication of the warlike career before him, that the swords jumped out of their scabbards and the muskets fired of their own accord on the night of his birth. His nurse, who possessed second sight, predicted that the child would become a great warrior, valiant and famous, and that victory would be his until the day that he planted his banner upon Gocam-gò. As possessing the mightiest arm in Ireland "a dh' aindeoin cò theireadh e," he, in 1644, was chosen leader of the Earl of Antrim's troops in support of Charles I. Alastair's successes with Montrose are a matter of history. One fine summer morning, while on the march through Argyll's country to chastise the Campbells, he halted for the morning meal. He asked the name of the green knoll over which his banner had been raised. " Gocam-gò " was the reply. Alastair remembered his nurse's warning, and the heart of the warrior who never yet turned his face from the foe (nor even scrupled to cut the head off an old friend if he happened to oppose his party) now became that of a child. After planting garrisons in Dunaverty and Dun Naomhaig, Alastair crossed over to Ireland, where soon afterwards he fell in battle.

Coll Ciotach took a leading part with Sir James M'Donald against the Campbells in 1615. He afterwards returned, unmolested, to Colonsay. While M'Phee occupied his stronghold of Dun Eibhinn, Coll resided in Kiloran. A feud for supremacy was carried on between these two hardy chiefs for the next six or seven years, until the murder of M'Phee. For many years after this event, Coll, with his family, lived on the island, and there is nothing in tradition to show that he was disliked by the people. The Campbells came down in force in 1639, and carried off everything that they could lay hands upon. From this date Coll's connection with the island became severed. He, along with his sons Gilleasbuig and Angus, is said to have supported Alastair at Inverlochy. He was afterwards treacherously entrapped by General Leslie outside the castle of Dun Naomhaig, and confined in Dunstaffnage. The old man was hung from his own galley mast over a rocky gully behind the castle.

After Coll Ciotach had been cleared out in 1639, Colonsay

apparently became a possession of the Campbells. In 1700 the island was sold by the Earl of Argyll to Donald M'Neill, the latter's estate of Crerar in South Knapdale being part of the purchase price. For the next 200 years Colonsay and Oransay remained in the possession of the M'Neills, many of whom, during that period, attained to distinction both in military and civil life. At the death of Major-General Sir John M'Neill, V.C., K.C.M.G., in 1904, the estate passed, by purchase, into the hands of the present proprietor, Lord Strathcona and Mount Royal, G.C.M.G., High Commissioner for Canada.

Most of the M'Neills now in Colonsay are descended from a person who, at an early date, migrated from the island of Barra. He, with his family and chattels, crossed the sea in an open boat. During the voyage his wife gave birth to a child, and to protect the mother and infant from the weather M'Neill slaughtered a cow and placed them in the warm carcase. The woman, a M'Phee, subsequently nursed one of the M'Phees of Colonsay, and by the turn of events we may assume that this was primarily the object of the migration. The child that was born in the boat was afterwards known as Iain a' Chuain (John of the Ocean), a designation that continued to be applied to succeeding generations of his descendants. M'Phee gave M'Neill a house at Baile Mhaide, some distance from the family residence. When M'Phee's cock happened to crow it was answered, after the manner of cocks, by M'Neill's. This assumption of independence, even by a fowl, so near her dwelling annoyed M'Phee's wife. To save further friction, the laird offered M'Neill his choice of any other place in the island as a site for a new habitation. M'Neill selected the place now known as Aird-an-Dùin, in Machrins, and there built his house, which continued to be occupied by many generations of his descendants. The badge of the M'Neills, white dryas (Machall Monaidh), does not grow in Colonsay, but it is found in some of the more mountainous northern islands. The local badge is Channelled Wrack (Feamainn Chireagach).

Although the monastery at Oransay is believed to have been founded originally by St Columba, the present buildings date from a much later period. St Columba's buildings were of clay and wattle, but even had they been constructed of more lasting material, it is certain that they would have been destroyed in the ninth and tenth centuries by the Vikings and the Danes. These hardy sea-rovers made their first descent on Iona in 795, and for the next 200 years our shores were subject to their invasions, often sudden and disastrous. The good John of Isla, Lord of the Isles, is credited with the foundation, about 1350, of the present priory at Oransay. It belonged to the Augustine order, and canons were brought from Holyrood.

While the Lords of the Isles were in power, Oransay, it may be assumed, was the centre of a flourishing community. Foundations have been traced which extended over a much larger area than the buildings now occupy. Along both sides of the road leading from the priory to the strand the ruins of a number of circular enclosures, each about 18 feet in diameter, are to be seen. Others were probably cleared away when the road was made. Those still existing are situated well within view of the church, and it is supposed that these structures had been used for stacking the seed-grain of persons living in Colonsay, who carried it across the strand for the blessing of the Church, and also for the more practical reason of having it preserved until seedtime from the depredations of freebooters. Oransay having the right of sanctuary was, so far, free from such visits.

A number of sculptured stones, some exhibiting very fine workmanship, are now arranged along one side of the chapel at Oransay. Formerly they lay on the floor, over the graves of persons of note, but for preservation they were removed to their present positions. One of the stones, on which is

carved in relief the figure of a knight in armour, is supposed
to have been to the memory of Sir Alexander M'Donald of
Loch Alsh, who was murdered in the prior's house in 1498 by
M'Ian of Ardnamurchan. The cloisters, which were described
by Pennant, have been partially restored. Of the many
crosses which once adorned the precincts of the priory, one
fine specimen is still standing. Hewn from a single stone,
it is fully 12 feet in height, and elaborately carved. It is
believed to have been erected to the memory of Colin, a
prior who died in 1510. Another cross (M'Duffie's Cross)
had been fixed in a cairn of stones on the way to the landing-
place. It is said that the bodies of the heads of the M'Duffie
family were rested for some moments on this cross as they were
taken to the chapel for burial.

The Iodhlann-mhor (large corn-yard) is a green, flat-topped
mound to the south of the priory. From excavations made,
it is believed that this was a circular enclosure formerly
used for stacking grain, and that the shifting sand gradually
filled it up and gave it its present striking outline. In the
course of excavations carried on in various parts of Oransay,
finds of antiquarian interest were obtained. Various
ornamental articles—bronze brooches and ring, beads, etc.
—were found in a grave at Carnan-a-Bharraich (Barra-man's
Cairn). The remains of animals, shellfish, etc., found in
an ancient kitchen-midden at Caisteal-nan-Gillean, and
enumerated by Mr Symington Grieve in his treatise on the
Great Auk (pp. 54, 55), indicate what the bill of fare of our
ancestors at different periods consisted of. Bones of the Red
Deer (Fiadh), Wild Boar (Fiadh Thorc; Cullach), Marten
(Taghan), Rat, Seal, and Otter [1] (Beist-Dubh; Dobhran),

---

[1] The Otter, at one time common, but absent from the island for
close on half a century, has recently been seen in the vicinity of its
old haunts at Port-na-Cuilce. Places in various parts of the island
—Rubha-an-Dòbhrain, Glaic an Taghain, Dunan-a-Chullaich, etc.—
are named after animals some of which have become extinct.

and those of various kinds of birds (including the Great Auk, an extinct species) and fishes, were identified. The Rabbit, though now plentiful in the island, is not indigenous, and is consequently not included as such in Mr Grieve's list. It is said that rabbits were first introduced from Barra in the eighteenth century, and that holes were dug for them in the sand-hills at Baile-Mhaide. The shellfish mentioned by Mr Grieve include the Oyster. Limpet-hammers, barbed bone spear-heads, lap-stones, and other articles were also found during excavations. Other shell deposits are to be seen at Cnoc Sligeach, Cnoc Riabhach, etc. Two places of interest not previously referred to in connection with Oransay are Cill-a-Mhoire, the site of an old chapel, and Dun Domhnuill, a conspicuously situated hill-fort with the ruins of rather extensive fortifications on the top.

Surrounding Oransay are a number of smaller islets and exposed reefs, congenial homes of the Cormorant (Sgarbh), the Eider Duck (Lacha Mhor), and many other sea-birds. In the winter time the scene is enlivened by the arrival of flocks of the Barnacle Goose (Cathan), Grey Lag Goose (Geadh Glas), Pintail Duck (Piobaire), and other visitors which are driven south from Northern Europe by the severity of winter. Seals of two kinds are numerous ; the large Grey Seal (Tabeist) preferring the solitude of the outer reefs, while the Common Seal (Ròn) is more frequently seen in the bays and channels nearer shore. Lying high and dry, beyond the reach of the tide, the young of the Grey Seal are to be seen on the rocky islets in late autumn. They are generally creamy white in colour, solitary, and lying motionless on the rocks, but showing signs of anger when approached. Helpless little creatures, too fat and buoyant for diving, they put their heads, in fancied security, under the water in times of danger. While they are still young their mothers are said to shift their

position at every spring tide. The Common Seal has its
young in spring and early summer.

Approached by steamer from the east it has been said that
"Colonsay has a barren, uninviting appearance, the shores
being rocky and often precipitous, and the prospect inland
being closed by bare, rugged hills. But the interior is
extremely fertile, showing wide stretches of pasture-land
and good agricultural farms."[1] The harbour is in the eastern
outlet of the more southern and lesser of two valleys
containing the bulk of the arable land, which cross the island
from side to side. In a prominent position on Cnoc-na-
Faire, overlooking the harbour, stands a granite obelisk
erected by the inhabitants to the memory of Lord Colonsay,
a former proprietor of the island and a well-known lawyer
of the Victorian era. He was Lord Justice General of
Scotland from 1851 to 1873, when he was created Baron
and made first Lord of Appeal from Scotland. Westward
from the harbour lie the farms of Scalasaig and Machrins ;
the latter extending to the western shore, and including
within its borders a well-situated golf-course. The mansion-
house, policies, and home-farm, and the crofting district
of Kilchattan occupy the greater portion of the northern
valley. In depressions among the hills in the north-
east and south of the island are other farms and crofting
townships.

A survey from a few points of vantage will discover that
the two valleys just referred to are closed in by three main
tracts of hills : one in the north, one in the centre, and another
in the south. The arable land is thus sheltered from cold
northerly winds, an important consideration from an agri-

---

[1] "Notes on the Geology of Colonsay and Oronsay," by James Geikie,
LL.D., F.R.S., F.R.S.E., etc., of H.M. Geological Survey (*Transactions of the Geological Society of Glasgow*, vol. vi. part ii., 1878-79,
1879-80).

cultural point of view. The hills decrease in elevation from north to south. They usually present their escarpments or steep faces to the north, falling with a gentler depression in the opposite direction. This formation is best seen north of Kilchattan and Kiloran, where the hills rise in perpendicular precipices from the sea, and gradually, though somewhat irregularly, slope southwards to Loch Fada. They rise again more or less abruptly from Loch Fada, falling with an easier gradient in the direction of Scalasaig and Machrins. These alternating ridges and valleys which cross the island from side to side are, to the popular mind, suggestive of a series of violent subterranean upheavals rather than the slower work of denudation.

Concurrently with an irregularity that appears in the rock structure in the north-east of the island, a series of ridges from Carnan Eoin to Beinn-na-Fitheach runs north and south at right angles to the main tracts of hills, effectively closing in the eastern gap of the main valley and sheltering Kiloran from withering easterly winds. Owing to the general conformation of the hills, cattle—for the rearing of which the island has long been famous—are able to find shelter from every wind that blows.

The largest sheets of fresh water are Lochs Fada and Sgoltaire; the former situated near the centre of the island, and the latter in the northern end. Marshy and reed-over-grown areas along their margins provide seclusion for water-fowl such as the Mallard or Wild Duck (Lacha Riabhach), Coot (Bolachdan), and Teal (Crann Lach). Winter visitors include the Widgeon (Lochlannach) and very occasional flocks of the Wild Swan (Eala Fhiadhaich). Numbers of Snipe (Gudabochd), and less commonly the Jack Snipe, inhabit the marshes. The Lapwing (Sadharcan) breeds plentifully in the peat-bogs on the north side of Loch Fada; and the Meadow Pipit or Titlark (Rèabhag), in whose nest the egg of the Cuckoo (Cuthag) has been

2

found, the Skylark (Uiseag), and the Land Rail or Corn
Crake (Tarritrèan) in the adjacent meadows. The idea
that the Corn Crake passes the coldest of the months in
holes in dry banks still survives. In winter the whistle
of the Golden Plover (Feadag) is heard in the surrounding
fields and commons.

On the north-western side of the island the hills overhang
the sea for some 3 miles, from Kiloran Bay to the Inbhear
in Kilchattan, in rugged, precipitous cliffs, rising here and
there in terraces, one above another, and interrupted at
intervals by chaotic accumulations of broken rocks, and by
deep and gloomy aoineadh's and slochd's. Most of this coast
is rock-bound, and inaccessible from the sea to all except the
daring and skilful lobster-fisher, who, to be successful in the
pursuit of his precarious calling, must know every treacherous
reef and every creek along the dangerous shore. North-
west of Kiloran Bay there are good examples of raised
beaches, platform-like in formation, and now forming the
arable land of the little crofts of Port-an-Tigh-mhòir.
Judging from the antiquarian remains, this now secluded
part of the island had, in former times, been a settlement
of some importance. Ruins of fortifications and buildings
curiously circular in outline are to be seen on the headland
of Cailleach Uragaig and at Dun Tealtaig. Cill-a-Rubha
is the site of an old church and graveyard. A corn-mill
or muileann-dubh, driven by the overflow water from
Loch Sgoltaire, is said to have been at one time situated
below Bealach-a-Mhuilinn. The only indication now re-
maining of the existence of this structure is a fragment of
a small millstone.

Westward, past Aoineadh-nam-Bà and the high precipice
of Geodha-gorm, is Aoineadh-nam-Muc, said in former times
to have been assigned by crofters as summer quarters for
their pigs to prevent them from roaming at large and damag-

ing the crops. Lamalum (Lambs' Holm), with its beautifully green verdured headland, its shingly beaches, and Piper's Cave, is a little farther on. Dreis-nic-Ceothain is named after a young woman who had the hardihood to walk across that dangerous ledge. In the cliffs around Aoineadh-nam-Muc, Lamalum, and other parts, great numbers of sea-fowl—Gulls of various kinds (Sgàireag = Kittiwake?, mostly) Cormorants, Guillemots (Eun Dubh a Sgadain), Razor-bills, etc.—lay their eggs on the ledges. When they are disturbed from their nests the shrill cries from thousands of throats, the howling of the wind over the edges of the cliffs, and the dashing of the waves beneath, create a discordance not readily forgotten. Binnean Riabhach, the highest sheer cliff (about 350 feet) in the island, is annually taken possession of by the Peregrine (Seobhag) for rearing its young; and as each spring comes round a pair of Ravens (Fitheach), in choosing a site for their nest, make a leisurely survey of the most inaccessible spots in the neighbourhood.

The sombre aspect of these northerly exposed and usually sunless cliffs is relieved from early summer onwards by an abundance of wild-flowers and ferns, which find root-space in the many interstices and on ledges in these broken and fast disintegrating rocks. Colonies of yellow-flowered Rose-root, glaucous green-foliaged Campion, rosy-coloured Thrift, daisy-like Matricary, together with the greenery of the Sea Spleenwort and many other plants and ferns, make a com-bination of pleasing colours that favourably contrasts with their rugged surroundings. Here also the Scottish Lovage and the rarer *Spergularia rupestris* are safe from the maraud-ing hands of the collector. Many other plants not usually characterised as sea-rock plants, and apparently happy in their novel surroundings on ledges and in crevices, lend a charm to the scene with their flowers of various hues. Among those noted were Bird's-foot Trefoil, Blue Scabious,

Honeysuckle, Stonecrop, Bramble, Lady Fern, Soft Meadow, Cock's-foot, and other grasses.

Kiloran Bay, with its much-admired stretch of yellow sand about a mile in width, is formed by a deep indentation in the northern coast-line. This neighbourhood, apart from its own peculiar attractions, is interesting botanically. A bed of sandy limestone, which, judging by the ruins of an old kiln near Craobh-na-Sgeachag, had at one time been burned by the inhabitants for making lime, accounts for the presence of certain calcicole or lime-loving plants. Hartstongue Fern is common in the gullies below Uragaig. Plants more or less confined to the neighbourhood are the curious little Moonwort Fern, Knotted Figwort, Sea Holly, and the Red Broomrape, which is parasitic on the roots of the Wild Thyme.

Natural sea-caves, haunts of the Rock Dove (Calman Creige) and other birds, penetrate into the rocks on both sides of Kiloran Bay for considerable distances. A number of fugitives are said to have been formerly suffocated by their enemies in the New Cave below Uragaig. Heaps of broken rocks and debris partly block the mouth of the cave. Inside there are a well and a smooth stone : the stone is said to have been used in former times by frequenters for sharpening their swords.

Slochd-dubh-Mhic-a-Phi is a natural tunnel in the rocks north of the New Cave, and the following traditional story in connection with it has been handed down for generations. A clansman of the Laird of Lochbuie who visited Colonsay was gleaning after the reapers in the Glen of Ardskenish ; and Macphee, the chief of the island, who was under a *geas* or taboo not to let pass a sword-stroke, coming round to see the shearers, when passing the Mull man cut off his hand. On finding this out, the M'Leans came over to avenge the deed. When he heard of their arrival, Macphee, accompanied by his servant and his famous black dog, left his

residence at Kiloran and escaped to the hills. As they were
retiring over Beinn-a-Sgoltaire they heard the wails of
Macphee's wife—herself a daughter of Lochbuie—who was
being maltreated by the M'Leans because she would not tell
them where her husband was hiding. Macphee exclaimed to
his servant: "Good were your promises to her the day she
gave you these trews," pointing to those that his servant
had on, "that you would see no harm come to her."
"Unlucky is the time that you remind me of it," answered
his henchman; "if I and the black dog were with you we
would defy them; but I will now return, and I shall be
slain, and you shall be caught also." Macphee, retiring to
the cave in question, which is open at both ends, set his
black dog at the one end while he took his stand at the
other, and both so well defended their respective posts that
it was only by opening a hole through the roof that the
M'Leans were able to get at them. This cave ever since
has been called Slochd-dubh-Mhic-a-Phì.

Bogha-Mhic-a-Bhàstair—a rocky islet, almost submerged
at high tide, on the western side of Kiloran Bay—is said
to have been named after one of Macphee's servants, who
landed on it to abstract an arrow with which he had been
pierced by his enemies while endeavouring to escape from
them by swimming across the bay. He pulled the arrow
out of his body, and swam over to Port Easdail; thence
walked to Port Olmsa, where he got a boat with which he
crossed the channel to Jura, and so escaped.

Place-names[1] and fragments of legendary lore would indicate that in former times raiding parties, who, judging by
the sequel in some cases, did not always fare well at the
hands of the inhabitants, sometimes landed at Kiloran Bay.

---

[1] It has been asserted that the places in Balanahard had formerly
been so well named in detail that the people without difficulty could
apportion the land out as they sat on Cnoc-a-Chreagain—"yes, even to
the breadth of a 'caibe' handle."

Lag-na-Birlinn, a slight depression on the west side of the blown sands, derived its name from an incident which ended with the burning of M'Lean's birlinn or barge. The boat must have been dragged through the dunes for about a quarter of a mile before it was set fire to. Rusty boat-rivets were found in the surface sands for many a long day after. Baile-Mhaide, some distance inland, is the reputed scene of an old-time conflict ; and here again the odds seem to have gone against the incomers, for their chief is said to have preferred voluntary death by drowning at Rudha-Buidhe-Mhic-Iomhair, on the east side of Balanahard, some 2 miles distant, rather than fall into the hands of his bloodthirsty pursuers. A well-preserved tomb of a Viking chief, with the skeletons of a man and horse, the metal parts of the horse's accoutrements, sword, balance, and other interesting relics now on view in the Royal Scottish Museum, were unearthed some years ago at Lag-na-Birlinn in the blown sands. The weights of the balance, which are of unknown value, are chased on one side, and are enamelled.

Balanahard comprises the north-eastern extremity of the island. Its northern shore-line is broken and precipitous. Off Meall-a-Chuilbh the sea, even in calm weather, is invariably agitated by the strong currents of the Gulf of Corryvreckan ; steamers here encountering more violent seas than those met off the dreaded Mull of Kintyre. In the cliffs around, the Scottish Lovage and the Rose-root grow in profusion. High up in the precipices of Slochd-a-Chroinn the Scurvy Grass is seen in great luxuriance, forming dense green masses. The Erect Bugle, a plant not previously recorded for this or neighbouring islands, was discovered on the syenite above Slochd-a-Chroinn.

Within living memory stone crosses, stone models of the human parts, and other relics of the past were to be seen at the ancient burying-ground of Cill Chatriona. At Cnoc Mhic 'Ille Mhinniche, near by, the crofters formerly followed a superstitious custom of pouring out, for good luck, an offer-ing of new milk when the cows were turned out to the fold on May Day. It was believed that if the practice was neglected by anyone, some evil would befall the delinquent's best cow. On one occasion, so it is related, an old woman who had accidentally spilt all her milk, gave an offering of whey instead. Appreciating the spirit, the dwellers under-neath struck up on the pipes the tune

> Fhuair mi deoch mhìg o'n mhnaoi laghaich
> Banarach nam bò, nach d'òl an cobhar.

Dun Loisgte, Dun Meadhonach, and Dun Crom, are close together on the north side of the farm ; Dun Leathann and Cnoc-na-Faire,[1] where the people in olden times used to watch for the approach of their enemies, lying to the south-east. The Cowrie Beach and Uinneag Iorcuil, a natural, window-like opening in one of the rocks, seen best from the sea, are in the extreme north-east. St Columba's, or the Wishing Well, is popularly credited with certain wish-fulfilling potentialities. Part of the ceremony is to leave a gift for the saint. A miscellaneous collection of articles is usually to be seen on the slabs which cover the well.

Bird life is varied and abundant among the rugged hills and secluded shores of Balanahard and the east of the island. The Carrion Crow (Feannag Dhubh), Grey or Hooded Crow (Feannag Ghlas), Buzzard (Croman), and Kestrel (Speireag Ghlas) here have their haunts. Among the broken rocks underneath the cliffs the Black Guillemot (Càlag) has its nest, and Mergansers (Sioltach) feed in pairs in the bays, building their nests in the heather in rocky places. The Jackdaw (Feannag Bheag), one of the farmer's pests, and

[1] There are at least two other hills (watch-hills) bearing the same name, one at Dun Ghaillionn and another at Scalasaig. Their situation in the northern end of the island indicates the direction from which the approach of their enemies was looked for by the natives.

the Starling (Druideag) inhabit clefts and fissures underneath Carnan Eoin. Woodcock (Coilleach Coille) nest among the withered bracken in the natural woods, from which also issues the prolonged jarring note of the Nightjar (Cuidheal-Mhor). Its nest, with two nestlings, has been found in the heather. To dry, stony, and lonely situations the Wheatear (Clachran) and the Stonechat are partial. In strange contrast with its wild surroundings, the little Rock Pipit appears flitting and chirping from rock to rock on the stormy shore.

Kiloran, with its pretty policies and plantations of forest trees, offers a pleasing contrast to the characteristic bareness of the surrounding landscape. "The luxuriance of the trees in the neighbourhood of Colonsay House astonishes the stranger, who, while wandering in their glades, might easily fancy himself in some well-wooded part of the Lowlands. Here we find growing vigorously in the open air, all the year round, several plants which on the mainland could not survive the winter." [1] The garden and grounds, which were laid out in a naturally well-sheltered situation, are now further protected by belts of forest trees. Plants, flowers, fruit, and vegetables usually seen in gardens on the mainland arrive here at a tolerable state of perfection.

The site of the present mansion-house adjoins that of an old abbey and churchyard. According to the *Old Statistical Account*, there was a monastery of Cistercians in the island, their abbey being in Kiloran and their priory in Oransay. At the beginning of last century the ruined walls of the old church, which stood on what is now a grassy slope southeast of the house, were removed to allow of the extension of the pleasure-grounds in that direction. In 1695 it is recorded by Martin that the "principal church" stood in the village of Kiloran. As early as 1549 Monro writes

[1] Professor Geikie, in his *Notes on the Geology of Colonsay and Oransay*.

that the island "hath ane parish kirke." Oran's Well, with
its unfailing spring of clear, cool (though possibly now
contaminated) water, is situated to the north-east of the
spot where the church stood. The abbey barn was utilised
for a time as mansion-house, retaining its designation of
"An Sabhall Bàn." It stood on the ground where the
kitchen-garden is now laid out; and here, according to
tradition, Montrose's famous general, Alastair Mac Colla
(Alexander MacDonald), son of Colla Ciotach (Kolkitto), was
born. Some stones at the base of an old elm are said to
have formed part of Coll's drying-kiln.

Among the ferns—Lady Fern, Male Fern, Broad Buckler
Fern, and others—luxuriating in the woods around Kiloran,
a few plants of the Soft Prickly Shield Fern, a rare
plant in the West of Scotland, were found. Gooseberries,
Raspberries, Currants, etc., carried from gardens, principally
by the Blackbird, are springing up everywhere. Besides
providing conditions suitable for the growth of particular
plants, those sheltered woods are the homes of numerous
birds that love a sylvan retreat. In spring and early
summer the Song Thrush (Smeòrach), Mistle Thrush (An
t-Eun Glas), Blackbird (Lon Dubh), Wren (Dreòllan), Red-
breast (Brudeargan), Titmouse (Cailleach a' Chinn Duibh),
and Chaffinch (Breac an t-Sìl) contribute to the chorus of
song. The Dipper (Gobha Dubh nan Allt), Water Rail
(Dreòllan Dorann), and Water Hen (Cearc Uisge) frequent
the burn and its vicinity. In the trees the Ring Dove
(Calman Coille) often has its nest; the Sparrow Hawk
(Speireag Ruadh) and Owl (Cailleach Oidhche) less frequently. Sparrows (Gealbhonn), which almost completely
disappeared, years ago, from the island, have again become
numerous and destructive to growing seeds—an occupation
that is being shared within recent years by the Greenfinch.
Small colonies of the Rook (Ròcais) attempted, unsuccess-
fully, on several occasions to settle in the trees in the park.

Other birds common in the vicinity and other parts of the island are the Wagtail · (Bigein an t-Sneachd), Hedge Accentor, and Yellow Bunting (Buidheag a' Chinn Oir). Less common species include the Bullfinch (Buidhean na Coille), Goldcrest, Tree Creeper, and Warblers.

Several other places in the neighbourhood of Kiloran are, on account of the traditions associated with them, worthy of passing notice. Dunan-nan-Nighean is on a low, somewhat isolated hillock to the south-east of Kiloran Bay. The entrance to the structure is in a more or less complete state, and still lintelled. The children of one of the chiefs of the M'Phees are said all to have been born here ; their mother removing hither from the family seat at Kiloran before the advent of each addition to the family. It is related that a number of daughters were born ; and there was a belief that if seven daughters were born in succession the seventh would be in possession of the second sight. Another version is, that in the event of a son being born in the Dun, he would be more fortunate than any of his race.

South of Kiloran, near the place where the road crosses between the eastern and middle portions of Loch Fada, a fight is alleged to have taken place between natives and Mull men, known since as Blar-an-Deabhaidh.[1] While the battle was in progress Calum Caol Mac Mhuirich (slender Malcolm M'Vurich), who lay ill of a fever in his house at Iodhlann Chorrach on the opposite side of the loch, had his servant on sentry outside keeping him informed of how it fared with the combatants. At last, getting excited, he impatiently donned his kilt, grasped his sword, and hurried across to join in the fray. He killed the first of the foe that he met ; and to instil a young native, whom he found hiding

[1] To assist in repelling the invaders, nineteen unbearded youths of the Bells (Cloinn Mhic 'Ille Mhaoil) alone, descended Bealach na h-àirde from Balanahard. Though at one time common, there is none now bearing the name in the island.

in a furze bush, with courage, he caught some of the gushing blood in the hollow of his hand and made the youth drink it. He then gave him a sword, and, inspired by Malcolm's example, the young man fought bravely until the invaders were vanquished. When the fight was finished, a friend, meeting Malcolm, remarked, " I thought you were ill with a fever." "Oh yes," he replied; " but I got relief." Return-ing homewards from Corra Dhunan, Malcolm noticed a reflection on the face of a rock some distance to the north of the middle loch, and on arriving at the spot found, to his surprise, eight of the foe lying fast asleep. Taking advantage of their helpless state, he killed them one after the other. He then collected their swords, which stood against a rock and caused the reflection which had first attracted his attention, and took his departure. This spot has ever since been known as Glaic-a-Mhoirt (Murder Hollow). Another version states that this incident took place on the following morning.

Ruins of hill-forts are not so common about Kiloran as in other parts of the island; and the remains of the few that are to be seen, such as Dunan-a-Chullaich, above the mill, and Dun Ghaillionn, half-way between Kiloran and Riskbuie, are in positions that are by no means unassailable. Another isolated knoll with traces of buildings on it, but now bearing no local name, situated to the south-west of Kiloran Bay, near Ceann-da-lèana, is better adapted for purposes of defence. Dunan Easdail is a small headland on the east side of Kiloran Bay.

Parts of the walls of the old church from which the town-ship of Kilchattan has derived its name are still standing, surrounded by the gravestones of the burying-ground, the only one that is now used in the island. The ruins of Cill-a-Mhoire, another of the old chapels, are to be seen east of the Baptist church. Two standing-stones—by some associ-ated with Druidical times—respectively 8 and 10 feet above the ground, and noticed by Pennant on his tour through the island in 1769, are conspicuously seen on the rising-ground between Loch Fada and Port Mor. Stone cists or coffins have been discovered in the cultivated ground near by. Dun Meadhonach, an isolated knoll to the south, formed the site of an easily defended fort.

The neighbourhood of Port Mor is botanically one of the most interesting in the island. The Wild Beet growing on the sea-rocks, Celery-leaved Ranunculus on the sandy shore, Parsley Dropwort at the edge of the brackish shore pools, and the tiny Lesser Duckweed floating on the surface of still waters, are among the local rarities not noticed elsewhere. In the little gullies of the rocky northern shore, amidst accumulations of shelly sand and decomposing seaweed, the glossy waving Sea Club-rush, the stout Foxsedge, and the slender *Juncus Gerardi* grow in great luxuriance.

While the country's trade overseas was still being carried on by sailing vessels, without lighthouses—of which four are now to be seen from Colonsay—to warn them of the proximity of dangerous rocks, hardly a winter passed without one or more wrecks taking place on some part of the island. The circumstances attending these losses are yet vividly recounted with more or less detail. Persons are living who witnessed the wreck of the barque *Clydesdale* on Eileannam-Ban at Port Mor during a storm in December 1848. Bound for Glasgow from Charleston in South Carolina with a cargo of cotton, the ship had been driven back, with sails torn, from the Mull of Kintyre by contrary south-easterly winds, which, veering westward, finally drove her on to the rocks. Though built a short time previously on the Clyde, of the toughest oak, the ill-fated vessel, under the pressure of the huge seas that dashed over her, soon broke in two. Twelve of the crew were rescued in fishing-boats by the natives, and others were saved by clinging to the stern portion of the vessel, but of the crew of twenty-three six men were drowned.

Machrins, to the casual tourist, is perhaps the best-known locality in the island, for lying along the shore between Maol Chlibhe and Druim Sligeach is that stretch of undulating machair land that holds such a fascination for the golfer, Machrins golf-links. Here, while he enjoys his game, the player may view a combination, on a small scale, of sea-coast scenery of bluff headland and receding sandy bay that is difficult to beat. Stretching out to sea and rising abruptly from the Atlantic, Dun Ghallain—named after Gallan, who was reputed to be a son of the King of Lochlann—formed an easily defended site for the fort that once crowned its summit. Flanked on either side by pretty sandy beaches— Traigh an Tobair Fhuair on the north and Port Lobh on the south—this headland was well adapted for defensive purposes.

From the ruins of the old fort at the top an extended view is obtained of the rock-bound coast from Kilchattan south beyond Ardskenish. Huge green seas rise over sunken rocks far out from shore, sometimes passing onwards with white and curling crests, sometimes breaking into surging masses of snowy foam. Bogha Sàmhach, one of the most treacherous of these sunken rocks, lies in the path of boats going north and south; the seas giving warning of its presence only by breaking occasionally and at unexpected moments. In the cliffs underneath the fort deep, gurgling caverns are grooved and worn by the ceaseless waves. Huge banks of rolled stones and gravel of every grade of fineness have been piled up by the Atlantic rollers at Rudha Aird-alanais and at Garbh Chladach. Inland, the golf-links and the arable land of Machrins form a pretty foreground of undulating sward backed in the distance by rugged and heath-clad hills; farther off, the outline of the misty hills of surrounding islands is seen.

Of the four ruined chapels observed by Pennant on his ride from Oransay to Kiloran, Cill-a-Bhrìde, situated about a quarter of a mile east of Machrins farm-house, was doubtless one, presuming he came from Oransay by the Temple of the Glen, and on to Machrins through Bealach-an-t-Sìthein. By this route the Temple of the Glen would be the first to be reached, Cill-a-Bhrìde the second, Kilchattan the third, and Kiloran the fourth. Had he chosen a more westerly course he would have passed Cill-a-Choinnich and Cill-a-Chiarain, thence going on to Kilchattan and Kiloran.

A Tigh Searmonachaidh ("preaching-house") stood at a little distance from the south end of Machrins farm-house, and served as the parish church until the present one was built in 1802, the minister's residence being then at Ardskenish. It was also called Tigh-na-Suidheachan from the fact that it was fitted with turf benches. The ruins have been long since removed to allow of the land in this part being cultivated. It was somewhere in this vicinity, too, that the earliest-known schools in the island had been situated; and one of the old school door-lintels with a schoolmaster's name carved on it was afterwards used as a corner-stone in the construction of a barn, now also falling into ruins.

Near the old church there was a "branks" (*brangas*) for the punishment of church offenders, who were usually pilloried during church service. It had been fixed to a large standing-stone, a part of which yet remains. The last person to be exposed to public odium in this way (according to one version) was a woman; and her brother, hearing of the occurrence, went out of church in indignation and released his sister. He then broke off the "branks" and threw it into Lochan Moine Nic Coiseam, "where it remains to this day."

"Latha Cath na Sguab air taobh tuath Dhun Ghallain "

was a well-remembered day in the annals of the locality, when a battle was fought on the sands of Traigh an Tobair Fhuair between natives and Norsemen, who, it is surmised, were attempting to land. The combatants on one side, probably the natives, appear to have been armed with sharpened sheaves of birch. That it turned out to be a deadly conflict for one side or the other, notwithstanding the primitive weapons in use, is proved by the number of human bones which have been exposed from time to time on the sands of the bay. There is a belief that if any one disturbs the bones by digging for lug-worms, the favourite bait in flounder-fishing, a storm will arise which will prevent the person from being able to use the bait thus obtained. It is a curious coincidence that the last time bait was dug here a storm came on which half-swamped the boat of those who set the lines.

Of the old ruins of Cill-a-Chiarain on the north side of Port Lobh hardly a vestige now remains, the stones having been used in building one of the field walls in the neighbourhood (gàradh na h-airde). Dunan-ga'-Gaoth is at the head of Traigh an Tobair Fhuair.

Following the old road southwards from Machrins through Druim Sligeach and down Bealach-na-Tràghadh, passing the deep gullies of Turnigil on the right and the grey Carna Glasa on the left, we come in view of the bent-covered dunes, the sandy beaches, and skerry-lined shores of Ardskenish. Cut off from Garvard by the bay of Traigh-nam-Bàrc on the east, this promontory, projecting for several miles into the Atlantic, forms the south-western extremity of the island. Stretching seaward for miles are reefs and sunken rocks over which the sea, as far as the eye can reach, rises in stormy weather into foaming masses of roaring breakers—an impressive sight of the power of the elements in an angry mood.

To the lover of nature these solitudes provide much that

is of interest. Seals bask lazily in the sunshine on the exposed reefs till the returning tide floats them off again. On the calm waters of Traigh-nam-Bàrc groups of Eiders may be seen congregating some distance from the shore. As these handsome birds often have their nests near the centre of the island and on the verges of high precipices, it is surmised that they carry their young, one by one, to the sea soon after they are hatched. Standing in the shallow waters of the Glen burn at the head of the bay, among less conspicuous members of their kind, are a few of the Great Black-Backed Gull (Dubh-Fhaoileann-Mhor). Sheldrakes (Cra-gheadh), handsomer specimens than their more domesticated brothers of the ornamental pond, anticipating danger, are shifting uneasily about in the vicinity of the sandbanks, in the rabbit-holes in which they often have their nests and lay a considerable number of eggs. Over mid-channel a pair of visiting Gannets (Amsan) are going through swift, lightning-like evolutions as they dive from a great height for the fish beneath. Nearer shore the elegant Tern (Stèirneal) imitates on a lesser scale the performance of the Solan ; not diving, however, but merely picking some delicate morsel off the surface of the sea. Among the wrack-covered boulders at the water's edge a Wild Duck affects the utmost incapacity for rational movement, which, as closer observation discovers, is only a device to draw away attention from a sadly reduced following of three ducklings, the remnant probably of a former lively brood of ten or twelve, a convincing proof of the rapacity of the voracious gulls. "Sandpipers" (Loirean Tràghadh) move briskly in search of insects along the sands, and a pair of Oyster-Catchers (Brìdein) manifest keen displeasure at the presence of the intruder by a steady volume of shrill and ear-piercing cries. Two dark-plumaged specimens of the Lesser Skua (Fàsgadair) are flying over the promontory in search of fresh victims. They chase and frighten the sea-gulls to make them disgorge their half-digested food, on which they, the "Gull-Teasers," subsist. Farther out to sea the Great Northern Diver (Bunabhua-chaille) disappears, when feeding, for several minutes at a time under the water. As we advance on our way along the shore an occasional Heron (Gorra-Ghriodhach), Curlew (Crotach), and wary Redshank (Coileach Tràghadh) rise with startled cry from sequestered hollows. The Lesser Black-Backed Gull (Dubh-Fhaoileann), Herring Gull (Faoileann Mhor), Black-Headed Gull (Aspag?), Common Gull (Faoileann Bheag), etc., are wheeling, with measured beat, along the shore, while various kinds of divers fish in the outer channels. Cormorants are particularly abundant, and it was formerly believed that they assumed a new stage of existence at the termination of every seven years :

> Seachd bliadhna 'na sgarbh,
> Seachd bliadhna 'na learg,
> Seachd bliadhna 'na bhal-ar-bòdhan,
> Gu sith-siorruidh 'na bhunabhuachaille.

Which may be translated thus :

> Seven years a sgarbh (Shag or Green Cormorant),
> Seven years a learg (young Cormorant ?),
> Seven years a bal-ar-bòdhan (Black Cormorant),
> For ever and ever a bunabhuachaille (Diver).

The Glen is a grassy flat closed in on the south-east side by the Garvard Hills, which rise abruptly over it in precipitous rocks. The soil—raised-beach deposits—is of a shelly, sandy nature, and produces wild flowers in abundance. A slow-flowing stream—Abhainn-a-Ghlinne—running parallel with the base of the rocks is the home of the Water Ranunculus, the Least Marshwort, and other aquatic plants. The elegant fern-like foliage of the Meadow-rue appears here and there from clefts in the rocks, and masses of the reddish-purple Hemp Agrimony and pink-tinged Valerian grow on the banks of the stream. The delicate white-flowered Grass of Parnassus is seen in profusion in moist places. Orchids in a variety of colours, blue Gentian, pink Centaury, orange Stork's-bill, and other free-flowering plants peculiar to such situations delight the senses with richness of colouring and sweetness of fragrance.

Garvard occupies the central part of the southern end of the island. The outlook among the islets of the strand is an ever-changing scene : at low tide, when the water recedes, wide tracts of shell-strewn sand are left exposed; at high tide, a land-encircled islet-studded sea, with the hills of Oransay in the background, lies before us. Memorials connected in traditional lore with interesting events in days gone by are not rare in this locality. Situated close to the road, about half a mile from the strand, are the partially standing walls of the Temple of the Glen, silent reminders of old ways that vanished together with the sway of the Romish Church at the advent of the Reformation. Local tradition associates the Temple of the Glen with a visit of King Robert the Bruce on the eve of his return to the mainland to reassert his right to the Scottish crown after his prolonged retreat in Rathlin ; and there is nothing improbable in the supposition that this vigorous monarch visited Colonsay and other islands, either on pilgrimage, or in the hope of winning over their hardy chiefs to his patriotic but desperate cause. In Sir Walter Scott's poetical narrative of the battle of Bannockburn in the *Lord of the Isles* Bruce is supported by a contingent of island chiefs under the leadership of the Lord of the Isles, and among these the Lord of Colonsay bears no inconspicuous part :—

> Brave Torquil from Dunvegan high,
> Lord of the misty hills of Skye,
> Mac-Niel, wild Bara's ancient thane,
> Duart, of bold Clan Gillian's strain,

Fergus, of Canna's castled bay,
  Mac-Duffith, Lord of Colonsay,
Soon as they saw the broadswords glance
  With ready weapons rose at once.

The shores of Mull on the eastward lay,
  And Ulva dark and Colonsay,
And all the group of islets gay
  That guard famed Staffa round.

Merrily, merrily, goes the bark,
  Before the gale she bounds ;
They left Loch-Tua on their lee,
  And they waken'd the men of the wild Tiree,
And the Chief of the sandy Coll.
  Lochbuie's fierce and warlike Lord
Their signal saw, and grasped his sword,
  And verdant Ilay call'd her host,
And the clans of Jura's rugged coast,
  And lonely Colonsay.

Yet still on Colonsay's fierce lord,
  Who press'd the chase with gory sword,
He (De Argentine) rode with spear in rest,
  And through his bloody tartans bored,
And through his gallant breast.
  Nail'd to the earth, the mountaineer
Yet writhed him up against the spear,
  And swung his broadsword round !
Stirrup, steel-boot, and cuish gave way,
  Beneath that blow's tremendous sway,
The blood gush'd from the wound ;
  And the grim Lord of Colonsay
Hath turn'd him on the ground,
  And laugh'd in death-pang, that his blade
The mortal thrust so well repaid.

Funeral parties on their way to Oransay halted at the
Temple of the Glen and there awaited the ebb of the tide
before crossing.   Half-way across the strand fragments of
lime-built stone-work show the foundation of the sanctuary
cross (Crois-an-Tearmaid) which marked the boundary of

the holy ground of Oransay. The criminal who got here before he was overtaken by his pursuers, and afterwards remained a year and a day in Oransay, was safe. Three dunans or small forts—Dunan-na-Fidean, Dunan Iochdar-na-Garbhaird, and Dunan-nan-Nighean, the last-named on the Ardskenish side beside Port-na-Patharlinn—are within view of one another on the southern shore; a fourth, Dunan-nan-Con, being situated close to the roadside farther north. Dun Cholla is a conspicuous green debris-covered hill on the Balaromin side, and was probably one of the larger, though at the same time one of the less easily defended, of the forts. A church had been situated at Cill-a-Choinnich, and a muileann-dubh stood beside the burn that has since borne its name on the Balaromin side of the strand. Cnoc Eibrigin, a conspicuous green knoll, is topped by a standing-stone of comparatively modern erection. It is said to have been the place where local questions and disputes used to be settled.

Two farms—Balaromin-dubh and Balaromin-mor—lie on the eastern side of the road that leads from Scalasaig to the strand. The dark heather-covered hills through which the road carries its winding, undulating way give place, towards the shore, to green slopes and fertile glades fringed here and there between projecting rocky points with pretty bays of white sand. Sycamore-trees, forming a rectangular square which surrounds the garden attached to the residence at Balaromin-dubh, have developed into fair-sized specimens, notwithstanding the open situation.

Lèana-na-h-Eaglais, or the Plain of the Church, is a flat of greensward near the farm-house of Balaromin-mor, with the remains of an enclosure surrounding the ruins of an old church. A short distance to the east there is a standing-stone to which Donald Ballach is said to have been bound before he was shot by the followers of Angus, son of the famous Coll Ciotach. At that time Colonsay was in the hands of the Marquis of Argyll, who sent Donald Ballach to the island as his representative. This individual taxed the very shellfish on the shore. On the death of the husband he claimed the horse or the cow of the widow. Sometime about 1644, Angus, son of Coll Ciotach, visited the island. He met a widow taking her only cow as a tribute (*damh-ursann*) to Donald Ballach. On hearing her story, Angus sent her home, saying that he would settle the matter with her oppressor. Accompanied by his men, he went to Oransay, where Donald Ballach was staying. The latter was at home on Angus's arrival, and he offered him snuff. " Have you a feather ? " (that is, for the snuff), asked Angus. " I have not," answered Donald Ballach ; " if I had [that is, the power of flying] I should not have been awaiting you here this night." Donald was dragged across the strand to Balaromin-mor, where his career was cut short by seven musket-balls ; and word was sent to the Marquis that if he sent another man like Donald Ballach to Colonsay he would be treated in a like manner.

On a clear day a fine view of the surroundings is obtained from the top of Beinn Eibhne, which rises abruptly from Poll Gorm to a height of 321 feet. Binnean Crom, a projecting shelf of rock over the edge of a precipice, is said to have been formerly used as a gallows for criminals. There is a hole in the shelf through which one end of the rope was passed. Ruins of old buildings are to be seen on the hill.

Underneath, on the rocky, sandy hillocks that fringe the shores of Poll Gorm, the Blue (and white) Spring Squill, the succulent-leaved Rockfoil, and the tidy Whitlow Grass grow in profusion.[1] Between Loch Colla and the sea there are stretches of marshy and boggy ground overgrown with characteristic peat-bog vegetation— Mud-sedge, Horse-tail, Bog-cotton, Club-rush, Spike-rush, Sun-dew, Bog Asphodel,

---

[1] Plants of salt-marsh—Glasswort, Milkwort, Sea Aster, and others —are abundant along the margin of the strand.

and many others equally common but bearing less familiar names.

Dun Eibhinn, situated about a mile west of the harbour, is one of the most impressive of the many forts that once crowned the summits of the hills throughout the island. It is circular in shape, and close on 100 feet in diameter. The position was practically inaccessible except on the side of the entrance to the fort. The hill, like a number more of those that had been utilised for defensive purposes, is green and strewn with the stones which had once formed the fortifications. The last of the M'Phees of Colonsay is said to have lived in the fort. Dunan Leathann is near Cnoc-an-Ardrigh, on the right-hand side of the road that leads up to Milbuie from Scalasaig. The stones were many years ago rolled down the slopes and used for building the dry-stone dyke on the east side of the road. The hearthstone (leac-an-teinntean) discovered in it was so large as to cause those who saw it to wonder how it could have been carried up the hill. A short distance from the hotel, in Buaile Riabhach, a Druidical circle is to be seen. On Beinn-nan-Gùdairean, to the south of Loch Fada, heather ale used, it is said, to be made. A large granite boulder, which was probably left there during the glacier period, lies near the top of the hill.

About a mile north of the harbour, at Riskbuie, on the east coast, some stones mark the site of the Caibeal—the Chapel of Riskbuie. A curious carved figure, now fixed up at Tobar Oran, was part of a stone cross formerly standing on the east side of the chapel. Another carved figure that rejoiced in the local sobriquet of Dealbh-na-leisg (Image of Sloth) is believed to have been built into one of the adjoining dwelling-houses.

In addition to those noted, other antiquarian remains—ruins, standing-stones, cairns, burial-places, knocking-stanes, etc.—are to be seen in various parts of the island.

Rare and Migrating Birds.—Birds rarely seen in Britain sometimes visit these islands, or are driven to them by stormy weather. One of these rare visitors was picked up alive at the roadside between Kiloran and Kilchattan on 1st January 1897. It was sent to Edinburgh, and identified by Mr W. Eagle Clarke, M.B.O.U., keeper of the Natural History Department, Royal Scottish Museum, as the Frigate Petrel. The bird is now on view in the Museum, and is one of the only two specimens yet found in European waters. The other one was washed ashore dead on Walney Island, Morecambe Bay, in November 1890. Prior to that date it was not seen north of the Canary Isles. Common in the Southern Hemisphere, the species was found breeding in great numbers on the islands off S.W. Australia by Gould's collector, Gilbert.

Certain birds, on the other hand, that used to frequent the island are now rarely or never seen. The Chough (Cnàmh-ach) used to nest in various places, but it has not been much in evidence for a number of years. From Sguid Pioghaid we might infer that the Magpie (Pioghaid) was once a native.

Visitors to the island or its shores that have been casually noticed include the Fieldfare (Liath-Truisg), Redwing, Shoveller, Tufted Duck, Sand Grouse (seen one season), Dotterel, Sanderling, Turnstone, Greenshank, Dunlin, and "American Cuckoo."

In addition to those already mentioned, the author has been able, with the kind assistance of Professor Graham Kerr, of Glasgow University, to bring together the local Gaelic and English (or Latin) names of various birds, fishes, shellfish, etc., which may be inserted here.

BIRDS.

Bal-ar-Bòdhan.—Black Cormorant.
Cathag.—Jackdaw. *Feannag Idheach.*
Clachran Coille.—Stone-chat.

Cearc Fhraoich.—Grouse.

Cearc Thomain.—Partridge.

Coileach Dubh.—Black Cock ; Black Grouse (male bird).

Coileach Fraoich
Coileach Ruadh } Moor Cock ; Red Grouse (male bird).

Eun-a-Ghiuirinn.—Puffin.

Eun-a-Phiocaich.—Black Guillemot in immature plumage.

Eun-Beag-a-Stoirm.—Stormy Petrel.

Eun-Mor.—Gannet ; Solan Goose. *Amsan.*

Faoileann Mhor Ghlas.—Applied probably to large species of Gull in immature plumage.

Geadh God.—Brent Goose.

Gearra Chrotach.—Whimbrel. *Cranna Chrotach.*

Iolaire.—Sea Eagle.

Lacha Mhor.—Eider Duck. Known in neighbouring islands as *Lacha Cholasach* (Colonsay Duck).

Learg Uisge.—The name given to the Black or Common Cormorant, when seen in winter fishing on fresh-water lochs or streams (see p. 33).

Liath Chearc.—Grey Hen ; Black Grouse (female bird).

Loirean (Gulamag).—Sandpiper.

Loirean Tràghadh.—Ring Plover and allied species.

Meana' Ghurag.—Snipe. Also *Gudabochd, Naosg.*

Seobhag Bheag Ghlas.—Merlin.

Sgarbh.—Shag or Green Cormorant.

FISHES.

Bacach-gearr.[1]—Turbot (?).

Bodach Ruadh.—Codling.

Bradan.—Salmon. *Liathag* = young Salmon or Grilse.

Bradan Leathan.[1]—Halibut (?).

Breac.—Fresh-water Trout.

Breac Donuis.—Shanny.

[1] The author, not having obtained specimens of these, is unable to identify them with certainty.

Cam-a-Reasain.[1]—Hag-fish (?). The Gaelic name is also applied to Fish-lice.

Carbhanach.[1]—Silver Smelt (?); Silver Haddock (?).

Càrnag.—A fish found at ebb-tide.

Carrachan.—Sea-scorpion, one of the Bullheads.

Clòimheag.—Butter-fish.

Cnamhairneich.[1]—(?).

Creagag.—Ballan Wrasse.

Crog Dhubh.[1]—Species of Bullhead (?).

Crùdan Dearg.—Gurnard (red).

Crùdan Glas.—Gurnard (grey).

Donnag.—Rockling (several kinds).

Easgann.—Eel.

Easgann Mara.—Conger.

Fionnag.—Whiting.

Garbhag.—Flounder.

Gealag.—Sea-trout.

Gibearneach. —Cuttle-fish.

Gobach Odhar.—A large kind of Ray or Skate.

Gobag.—Dog-fish.

Greusaiche.—Father-lasher (?), a species of Bullhead or Gurnard.

Iasg-Mear.—Grey Mullet.

Langa.—Ling.

Lèabag.—Flounder. *Garbhag* (local).

Lèabag Bhuinn.—Sole.

Lèabag Mhor.—Diamond Plaice. *Lèabag* (local).

Liù.—Lythe ; Pollack.

Mac-làmhaich.—Devil-fish ; Octopus.

Morair.—Haddock. *Adag.*

Mùrlach.—King-fish (local); Lesser Spotted Dog-fish.

Nathair Thràghadh.[1]—Pipe-fish (?); sometimes applied to Rag-worm.

[1] The author, not having obtained specimens of these, is unable to identify them with certainty.

Ordag-a-Mhuilleir. — Gemmeous Dragonet, one of the Gobies.

Piocach.—Saithe ; Coal-fish. In its young state it is known as *Cudainn* (Cuddy) ; in the May following, *Céiteanach. Piocach* is applied to it in the second year, and *Piocach-mòr* after. *Ucsa* is the mature fish.

Rionnach.—Mackerel.

Rionnach-an-Eich.—Horse Mackerel.

Sgadan.—Herring.

Sgat.—Ray ; Skate.

Siolag.—Launce ; Sand-eel (local).

Sporran Feannaig.—Mermaid's Purse : the egg of the Dog-fish or a species of Skate.

Suil Oir.[1]—Poor Cod (?).

Trosg.—Cod.

SHELL-FISH, ETC.

Bairneach.—Limpet.

Breallascan.—Gaper Shell.

Ciochan-nam-Ban-Marbh.—Sea Anemone.

Claba Dubha.—*Cyprina Islandica.*

Cluasag Baintighearna.—(*Artemis exoleta.*)

Conachag.—Buckie ; Whelk.

Conan Mara.—Sea Urchin.

Crùban.—Partan ; Edible Crab.

Deargann Tràghadh.—Sand-hopper ; Sand-flea.

Deiseag.—Velvet Swimming Crab.

Eisir.—Oyster.

Faochag.—Periwinkle ; Whelk (local).

Fèasgan.—Mussel.

Fèasgan-mor.—Horse Mussel.

Figheadair Fairge.—Spider Crab (?) with long limbs.

Gailleag.—Cockle.

---

[1] The author, not having obtained specimens of these, is unable to identify them with certainty.

Gille-geal.—White Whelk ; Dog-winkle.

Giomach.—Lobster.

Giomach Dearg.—Spiny Lobster.

Giomach Tuathalach.[1]—(?).

Giuirinn.—Barnacle.

Gorra-Cràg.—Star-fish.

Luga.—Lug or Lob-worm.

Maighdeag.—Cowrie Shell.

Muisgeann.—Razor-fish ; Spout-fish.

Partan.—Green Shore Crab.

Partan Tuathalach.—Scorpion Spider Crab.

Sgeith Ròin.—Jelly-fish.

Slige Cas Capuill.—Sometimes applied to the flat shell of the Clam.

Slige Chreachain.—Scallop Shell ; Clam.

Sop-gun-Iarraidh.—The spawn of the Whelk or Buckie.

SEAWEEDS [2]

Barr Dearg.—Tangle tops.

Barr Leathachan.—*Laminaria saccharina.* Sea-belt.

Cailionnagach.—*Plocamium coccineum.*

Carrachdag ; Dubh-Shlat. — *Laminaria digitata,* var. *stenophylla.*

Duileasg.—Dulse.

Feamainn.—Seaweed ; Sea-ware.

Feamainn Bhuiceanach.—*Fucus platycarpus* (*F. ceranoide*s).

Feamainn Bhuidhe.—*Fucus nodosus.* Knobbed Seaweed. This was the kind formerly used (locally) for making kelp. It was cut every third year.

Feamainn Bhuilgeanach.—Bladder Wrack (*Propach,* C.).

---

[1] The author, not having obtained specimens of these, is unable to identify them with certainty.

[2] For kind assistance in the identification of the Seaweeds, the writer's thanks are due to Miss Zamorska, Technical College, Glasgow.

Feamainn Chireagach.—Channelled Wrack.

Feamainn Dhubh.—*Fucus serratus.* Notched Wrack.

Gille-ma-Lionn.—Sea Laces.

Gruag-na-Maighdean-Mhara.—*Desmarestia aculeata.*

Lìobhagach.—Applied to Confervæ such as *Enteromorpha intestinalis,* etc.

Mathair-an-Duilisg.—Carrageen ; Irish Moss.

Muraille.—Badderlocks ; Henware ; Murlins. The midrib and the spore-producing part of it (*Sgeachagan*) are edible.

Muraille-mòr.—*Himanthalia lorea* (female plant).

Ròmhagach.—*Himanthalia lorea* (male plant).

Slabhachdan.—Sloke.

Stafa.—*Laminaria digitata.* Tangle.

Tràilleach.—A kind of seaweed considered to be of little value as manure for land, as it dried up and took a long time to decay.

CHAPTER II

The occurrence in the Western Islands of Scotland of certain plants — Rock Samphire, Sea-Kale, etc.—confined elsewhere in Europe to countries lying farther south, points to more equable conditions of climate than have been generally supposed to prevail in these northern latitudes. The Rock Samphire was found in Colonsay in 1906, and two years later on the Mangustra cliffs, a little north of Eilean Molach, on the west coast of Lewis, in lat. 58° 5′ N. On the authority of Mr Bennett, no station for this plant, outside Britain, is known in Europe north of lat. 51°. The Sea-Kale occurs in Islay, and there is an old record of the finding of it in the Outer Hebrides—"head of Lochmaddy, North Uist, on sand, 1848. D. C. Burlingham."

From the returns of the meteorological stations (as they are printed in the Journals of the Meteorological Society), we find that the Western Islands of Scotland possess a climate which, in mildness and uniformity of temperature, is quite exceptional, and without a parallel in the same latitude. During the months of December and January the mean temperature of those islands lying south of Harris and Skye—41° to 44° F.—is reached or exceeded elsewhere in Britain only in the Isle of Man and Anglesea, and in the western and south-western extremities of England and Wales. The only places in Scotland with a mean tempera-

ture of not less than 42° F. during January are the southern
islands of the Outer Hebrides—North Uist, Benbecula, South
Uist, and Barra, with their islets, and Tiree in the Inner
Hebrides.   Thus we find tender exotics, unable to survive the
keener winters of the neighbourhood of London, thriving
in the Western Islands, much farther north.

The influences at work in modifying the cold of winter
are equally well marked in tempering the heat of summer.
During the warmest months—June, July, and August—
the only districts in the kingdom that have a mean temperature as low as, or lower than, that of the Isles—53° to
57° F.—are the seaboards of Argyll and Western Inverness,
a narrow strip along the north-east of Scotland to Kinnaird
Head, and the counties lying north of the Moray Firth.   As
an agreeable change from the warmer and more enervating
regions of the south, the cool, bracing climate of the Islands
is yearly becoming more appreciated by an increasing number
of tourists, who travel westwards during the warmest of the
months.

The mildness of the Hebridean climate is emphasised by
taking a wider view of the subject, and comparing the
climate of the country as a whole with that of other
countries in the same latitude.   The following table, repro-
duced from Hann's *Climatology*, shows the

MEAN TEMPERATURES ALONG LATITUDE 52° N. FROM
WEST TO EAST

Station.	Longitude.	January.	July.	Difference.
Valencia, S. W. Ireland .	10° 25′ W.	42°·3 F.	59°·2 F.	16°·9 F.
Oxford	1° 16′ W.	38°·5	61°·2	22°·7
Posen	17° 5′ E.	27°·1	64°·9	37°·8
Kursk	36° 8′ E.	15°·1	67°·6	52°·5
Barnaul and Semipala-				
tinsk. . . .	80° 30′ E.	− 0°·4	71°·2	71°·6

Formerly the mildness of our winters was generally attributed to the influence of the Gulf Stream, which was supposed to flow across the Atlantic in a never-ending stream of warmer waters to our shores. This long-established theory has of late years lost its weight with many investigators. It is found that the Gulf Stream has almost ceased to exist a little to the east of the Banks of Newfoundland; and the most recent authorities attribute the favourable temperature conditions of the North Atlantic directly to the influence of the prevailing south-westerly winds, and indirectly to a surface drift of warmer waters which these winds drive before them. The prevailing winds on the American side of the Atlantic, on the other hand, are from the north-east, bringing to lower latitudes the icy conditions of the Arctic Circle. The prevalence of our balmy south-westerly winds is due to the existence of a permanent area of high pressure near the Azores, and a permanent area of low pressure near Iceland.[1]

Although no record of the climate of Colonsay is available, an approximate idea of its character may be formed from the returns of surrounding meteorological stations (*v.* p. 48). The island's vegetation is also a good indication of the nature of its climate, and if we had no other means of information much could still be learned, with regard to the general meteorological conditions prevailing, from a careful survey of the island's flora. Moss- and lichen-coated trees indicate a moisture-laden atmosphere; spongy and mossy pastures, and an abundance of rushes, sedges, and other plants of wet situations point to an unstinted and a well-distributed rainfall. Trees and plantations leaning east-

---

[1] "Address on the Climate of the British Isles," by Andrew Watt, M.A., F.R.S.E., Secretary of the Scottish Meteorological Society (*Scottish Geographical Magazine*, April 1908). Much of the information herein contained has been gleaned from Mr Watt's interesting paper.

TABLE SHOWING THE MEAN MONTHLY AND ANNUAL TEMPERATURES
OF THREE INSULAR STATIONS SURROUNDING COLONSAY: those
for the first and second being calculated on a mean of 40 years—
January 1856 to December 1895—and for the third on a mean of
10 years—1897 to 1906 inclusive.

Station.	Elevation.	Distance and Direction from Colonsay.	January.	February.	March.	April.	May.	June.
Rudha Vaal, Islay . .	feet. 147	miles. 8 S	40·9	40·3	40·9	45·0	48·6	54·2
Du Hirteach Lighthouse	145	15 WNW	42·0	41·4	41·9	45·0	48·3	52·9
Lochbuie, Mull . .	20	20 NE	43·1	39·0	41·0	44·6	49·3	55·4

Station.	Elevation.	Distance and Direction from Colonsay.	July.	August.	September.	October.	November.	December.	Year.
Rudha Vaal, Islay . .	feet. 147	miles. 8 S	55·6	56·0	54·0	48·9	44·5	42·7	47·9
Du Hirteach Lighthouse	145	15 WNW	55·2	55·7	54·4	49·1	45·5	44·0	48·0
Lochbuie, Mull . .	20	20 NE	57·0	56·4	54·5	48·4	44·6	41·5	47·9

ward testify to the prevalence and force of the westerly
winds. Plants of foreign origin, which are found growing
extensively out of doors elsewhere only in the climatically
favoured counties of Cornwall and Devonshire, indicate the
mildness of the island's winter climate. In favourable
seasons, the peach and the fig ripen their fruit in good
situations on walls in the open. The heat of summer is
not, however, sufficient, as a rule, to bring wheat to perfec-

tion; and owing to the prevalence of sunless days in autumn the ripening process of the young wood of fruit-trees and other plants is often but imperfectly done.

Temperature.—According to Dr Buchan's maps of the temperature of the British Isles, the mean annual temperature of the county of Argyll is 48°·5 F. ; the average variation being 39°·5–42° F. in January to 56°–57°·5 F. in July.

In mid-winter (January) the only parts of Britain that have a mean temperature of 41° F. and over are situated west of a line drawn from Loch Roag in Lewis southward through Skye, Ardnamurchan, and the Isles of Mull and Islay. Colonsay lies west of this line, with, if it be produced farther south, the Isle of Man and Anglesea, the western seaboards of Wales and the extreme south-western counties of England. Along the East Coast, on the other hand, the isotherms of 38° and 39° are dominant. In mid-summer, again, we find that, owing to the tempering influence of the Atlantic, the temperature on the West Coast is generally lower than it is on the East.

Elevation and Temperature.—For every 300 feet ascent that we make the thermometer drops 1° F. To get the same decrease of temperature at sea-level we have to travel more than a degree of latitude due north. Owing to this natural decrease of temperature from south to north, we find that the limit at which cultivation can be carried on gradually descends from an altitude of 2000 feet in the south of England to sea-level in the Shetland Isles. The bracken is said to determine the line of cultivation in Britain, but on the West Coast it is not uncommonly found growing at elevations at which few crops could be grown with profit. In a low-lying island like Colonsay, the difference in temperature between sea-level and the highest point is so small (less than 2° F.) as to be barely noticeable, and hardly sufficient to affect the distribution of plants. On the mainland, however, and wherever the land attains to a considerable altitude, we find,

4

as we ascend, an appreciable reduction of temperature, marked
in the loftier of the islands by the occurrence of certain species
of plants that are rarely, or never, found growing at low levels.

Rainfall.—According to Dr Hugh Robert Mill, Director
of the "British Rainfall," the yearly rainfall of Colonsay
may be taken as varying from 40 to 50 inches, distributed
throughout the months of the year, on an average, as
follows :—January 5 inches, February 4 inches, March
3 inches, April 2 inches, May 2 inches, June 3 inches, July
4 inches, August 4 inches, September 5 inches, October
5 inches, November 5 inches, December 5 inches.

MEAN MONTHLY AND ANNUAL RAINFALL OF THREE INSULAR
    STATIONS SURROUNDING COLONSAY : calculated on a mean of
    15 years—1876 to 1890—for Gruinart and Fladda, and on a mean
    of 9 years—1866 to 1874—for Hynish, Tiree.

Station.	Elevation.	Distance and Direction from Colonsay.	January.	February.	March.	April.	May.	June.
	feet	miles						
Gruinart, Islay	214	10 S	4·88	3·55	3·11	2·07	2·09	2·86
Fladda . .	12	20 NE	6·66	4·28	4·10	2·35	2·50	3·74
Hynish Farm, Tiree . .	50	34 NW	5·27	3·53	2·90	2·63	2·26	2·19

Station.	Elevation.	Distance and Direction from Colonsay.	July.	August.	September.	October.	November.	December.	Year.
	feet	miles							
Gruinart, Islay	214	10 S	3·07	3·80	4·33	4·25	4·98	5·41	44·40
Fladda . .	12	20 NE	4·19	4·36	5·14	5·48	6·27	5·82	54·89
Hynish Farm, Tiree . .	50	34 NW	3·18	2·73	4·18	4·32	3·86	3·47	40·52

The height and configuration of the land have a powerful influence on the rainfall. Where high hills intercept moisture-laden winds from the sea, the fall is much greater than it is in low-lying districts. Warm air holds more vapour in suspension than cold air; and as the moisture-laden winds that blow in from the sea rise over the hills they quickly cool and precipitate part of their moisture in the form of rain or fog. At the low-lying lands of the Rhinns of Islay the average fall is probably under 40 inches; in the more hilly district round M'Arthur's Head in the same island it rises to about 60 inches (37 years' average, 1862-98). In Tiree, where much of the land is scarcely higher than sea-level, the annual fall is little more than 40 inches; at Lochbuie, which lies under the high mountains of Mull, it is 90 inches. At Stornoway the annual fall is about 48 inches (1856-98), at Portree 88 inches, and at Dunollie and Oban about 60 inches.

A comparison of the returns from the East Coast with those from the West shows that the rainfall on the West Coast is much greater than it is on the East, on no part of which does it reach 40 inches, while it is less than 30 on the north-east coast of Caithness, the low-lying lands to the south-east of the Moray Firth, along the East Coast to Burntisland, and on the low grounds of Mid and East Lothian. Over a large part of the south-east of England, from the Humber to the estuary of the Thames, the average rainfall varies from about 22 to 25 inches. The average number of days on which rain falls annually on the West Coast is about 200, and on the East Coast 150. Great variations, however, occur in the annual rainfall, and a short series of observations, if taken as indicating the average rainfall of a particular district, might prove very misleading. Even a decade is not a long enough period to get a true mean. The seventies were a wet decade, which, if taken alone, would lead us to overestimate the rainfall of many localities; the eighties, a dry decade that would cause us to underestimate it.

Winds.—In the more exposed of the Western Isles the prevalence of strong winds has a most detrimental effect on the growth of many plants, particularly those that are not native but have been introduced to the islands. During the early part of the growing season the tender leaves and shoots of trees in exposed positions become prematurely battered and brown, and are rendered unfit for carrying on the complicated processes that are so vital to the well-being of the plant. Not infrequently the young leaves are torn off the trees by the force of the wind before they are fully developed. Owing to the preponderance of westerly winds, trees in exposed positions acquire a characteristic one-sided shape, the greater part of their development being in the easterly direction. Autumn gales frequently damage the fruit crop by stripping the fruit off the trees. Often when a gale or stormy weather is approaching from the west a rising swell on the sea gives premonitory warning of its advance several days beforehand, even though the air around may be comparatively still.

Directions from which the wind blew at Du Hirteach Lighthouse (15 miles W.N.W. of Colonsay) during 1898 :— N., 44 days; N.E., 19 days; E., 28 days; S.E., 37 days; S., 58 days; S.W., 69 days; W., 59 days; N.W., 49 days; calm or variable, 2 days.

Sunshine.—The percentage of sunshine on the West Coast is greater than might be expected, taking into consideration the heavy rainfall of the West Coast when compared with that of the East. In 1906 bright sunshine at Oban was 28 per cent (average rainfall 60 inches), and in Edinburgh 31½ per cent (rainfall 26 inches). The average sunshine for Stornoway for 25 years is 29 per cent. In spring, when east winds are common, the West Coast is frequently much sunnier than the East. Locally, the sunniest and driest weather is experienced in the months of April, May, and June, crops sometimes suffering from drought during that period.

In the daily sunshine returns for May and June 1909, published from health and holiday resorts all over the country, Oban, for a period, remained at the top of the list. In addition to this remarkable duration of sunshine, the climate of the district is characterised by other notable features. Analysis has shown that, for purity, its atmosphere is unexcelled in Europe; and while all along the West Coast the rainfall is considerable, the humidity is less than that of Brighton and other health resorts in the south of England. The dryness of the atmosphere in Colonsay may be gathered from the rapidity with which the soil and the roads dry even after heavy rains.

Temperature of the Sea.—The mean annual temperature of the sea on the West Coast of Scotland is 49°·1 F., ranging (at Oban) from 43°·3 F. in March (the coldest period) to 55°·7 F. in August. In shallow bays, at full tide on a sunny day, the temperature is much higher, and in Colonsay the sea is much warmer on the southern than it is on its deeper northern shores. On the East Coast of Scotland the mean annual temperature of the sea is 1° to 2° F. less than that of the West, ranging (at Dunbar) from 40°·3 F. in March to 56°·4 in August. The temperatures of the sea and the air are about equal on the East Coast; on the West Coast the temperature of the sea is 2° to 3° F. in excess of that of the air.

CHAPTER III

VIEWED across the intervening channel from Colonsay, the landscape of Mull presents to us certain unfamiliar features which find no counterpart in Colonsay or in any of the neighbouring islands within view. The terraced outline of the majestic Ben Mor is rounded and full, but, even where dissected into summits and slopes, this Tertiary volcanic mass differs fundamentally in appearance from the hills of the southern islands, which are composed of very ancient schistose rocks.

In these two islands, Colonsay and Mull, we have types sufficiently illustrative of the two main formations—schistose and gneissose on the one hand, and basaltic on the other—into which the Western Isles of Scotland may be grouped. Colonsay, Gigha, Islay, Jura, and neighbouring islets are, as might be expected from the trend of the great Caledonian rent, closely associated in structure with the mainland of Argyll. It is not certain, however, that the rocks of Colonsay are actually represented among the schists of the Argyllshire mainland, and it is interesting to note that Dr Peach places them in the great Torridonian system, named after Loch Torridon in Ross-shire. The rocks of Coll, Tiree, Iona, and the Outer Hebrides are more like the north of Scotland gneisses. Skye, Canna, Eigg, Mull, and some smaller islets comprise those of basaltic structure.

While broadly placing them in a few groups, minor

differences enter into the formation of individual islands which impart to each its distinctive characteristics in landscape and scenery; the composition of the flora also varies to some extent. Few of the islands of the Inner Hebrides are, in detail, identical in structure; but the Outer Hebrides present us with more of a sameness in formation, their entire length, a stretch of 130 miles, being mainly composed of Old or Lewisian gneiss, the most ancient rock in Britain. Coll, Tiree, and the greater part of Iona are similarly formed. In some of the Outer Hebrides, where the vegetation is too scanty to obscure its naked surface, this rock imparts a barren and desolate aspect to the landscape. It attains its greatest elevation in the island of Harris, where it rises to a height of 2662 feet.

The basaltic islands, from Skye southward to Mull, are of much more recent origin, and consist of consolidated lava-flows erupted during the Tertiary period. Ulster, Mull, Rum, Skye, St Kilda, the Faroes, and Iceland are believed to have been the principal centres of volcanic activity, from which, it is claimed by some, cones arose to a height of 15,000 feet, ejecting discharges which overran an area of 40,000 square miles. Others hold that the lavas issued more often from fissures than from definite craters, and built up undulating plateaux rather than cones. The numerous north-west basaltic "dykes" of the Western Highlands furnish ample evidence of the existence of volcanic fissures of this period, although it remains an open question whether these were the chief sources of the lava streams. There is no lack of evidence to show that these islands were once united in one great plateau.[1]

The northern and larger portion of the Isle of Skye is mainly composed of Tertiary volcanic rocks. The Cullins originated from bosses of gabbro which pierced through underlying basalt plateaux; and the Red Hills between

[1] See Appendix.

Sligachan and Broadford have been similarly formed of granophyre and allied rocks—striking examples of the peculiar contour assumed by the particular varieties of rock of which they are composed. There are large areas of Torridonian sandstone, much like that of Colonsay, in the south of Skye; and the neighbouring isles of Soay, Scalpay, and part of Raasay are mainly formed of it.

Torridonian sandstone is the principal rock in the northern half of Rum. The higher mountains of the southern portion of the island are composed of gabbro. Quartz-porphyry and allied rocks enter into the formation of the western side; while gneissose rocks, recently shown by Mr Harker to be of Tertiary age, are much in evidence in the south-east. The isles of Canna, Muck, and Eigg mainly consist of basaltic lavas.

Mull, like the northern part of Skye, is mostly Tertiary volcanic rock. Deep layers of lava flows appear to cover remains of the Mesozoic period. The mountains north of Lochbuie are composed of gabbro; while Ben Mor, the highest mountain in Mull, is formed of bedded lavas. Granite appears over a large area of the Ross of Mull. It is quarried, and has been largely employed in structures requiring great strength. Du Hirteach and Skerryvore lighthouses, Blackfriars Bridge, Holborn Viaduct, Thames Embankment, and the Prince Consort Memorial, Hyde Park, are well-known structures for which this stone has been used.

The landscape of the basaltic differs greatly from that of the gneissose and schistose islands. The regular terraced formation and beautiful green-verdured slopes, such as are to be seen in Mull and the north of Skye, pleasingly contrast with the irregular ruggedness of the Outer and South Inner Hebrides. As the decay of the rocks furnishes a rich loam which supports a luxuriant growth of grass, the basalt districts are distinguished by their greenness even up to the tops of the hills.

The South Inner Hebrides consist, for the most part, of a series of complicated and highly metamorphosed rocks, known for the present as Dalriadian, from the ancient Celtic kingdom of Dalriada. The islands form, as it were, the south-western fringe of the zone of rocks belonging to this group, which traverses the Central Highlands of Scotland. Gigha, the most southern of the islands, is, like the adjacent portion of Kintyre, mainly composed of quartzite and mica-schist. The western part of Islay consists mostly of grits and dark slates of the Torridonian system, with Lewisian gneisses forming the Rhinns. The central parts are mostly slate, the north and east quartzite-schist. Broad belts of limestone run between Portaskaig and the head of Lochindaal. Portaskaig is well known to geologists also for its conglomerates containing granite boulders. Jura and Scarba are principally formed of quartzite-schist. The Paps of Jura and the adjacent hills of Islay are among the finest and most characteristic examples of quartzite rocks to be seen in the Highlands. Luing and Seil are composed of graphitic mica-schist and black slate, the latter being worked ; Lismore and the Garvelloch Isles consist of lime-stone, associated in the latter with Portaskaig conglomerate ; Kerrera is composed of andesite (porphyrite), etc.

The islands of Colonsay and Oransay were described by M'Culloch as " extremely uninteresting in a geological view," the predominant rock being micaceous schist ; but subsequent investigations have discovered that there are other and interesting varieties of rock entering into the structure of these islands. Quite recent researches, by Messrs Wright and Bailey of the Geological Survey, have brought to light certain facts which may have an important bearing, not only on the orogenic history of Colonsay, but also on that of the Highlands in general.

Geology, to the lay mind, is a somewhat abstruse subject,

and it is not proposed here to enter into its discussion further than to note some of its relations to the landscape and flora of Colonsay. The difficulties encountered by any other than a geologist in tracing certain rocks through the island, owing to the superficial resemblance the different varieties bear to one another and their lack of distinctive features, are greatly increased by the many intermediate forms which they assume. Irregularities in topography and in the outcropping of the rocks also occur, which are sufficiently great to perplex the novice in his pursuit of practical geology in the field, and to prevent him, if left to his own resources, from ever discovering the key to the stratigraphical problem of the islands. A coloured geological map, kindly lent by Messrs Wright and Bailey, prepared after the recent survey of the island by the Geological Department, enabled the writer to follow up the principal rocks throughout the island, with a view to ascertaining the influence (if any) exerted by the underlying strata on the surface vegetation, referred to more in detail elsewhere.

Colonsay and Oransay are, as already stated, mainly composed of sedimentary rock of Lower Torridonian age. They consist of "alternating series of grits, flags, and mud-stones, with a well-marked bed of sandy limestone near the top."[1] The strike is approximately north-east and south-west, and the prevalent dip towards the east. "The Colonsay limestone, which, with the beds above and below it, constitutes an easily recognisable horizon, occurs on the eastern coast of the island, dipping out to sea at a low angle." An almost continuous succession from higher to lower beds is passed over as one proceeds westwards or southwards from the limestone, " and on finally reaching the extreme outlying parts of Oransay and Ardskenish there is still no indication

[1] "The Two Earth-Movements of Colonsay," by W. B. Wright, B.A., F.G.S. (*Quarterly Journal of the Geological Society*, vol. lxiv. No. 254, p. 297).

of any base to this enormously thick series of sediments."
Taking the harbour, therefore, as the most accessible though
perhaps not the most illustrative starting-point, and following
the road westwards past Machrins beyond the golf-links to
Dun Ghallain, some 3 miles distant, we may conveniently
take note of the principal series of strata of which the
island is composed as they occur on the way.

In the immediate neighbourhood of Scalasaig there is a
mass of granitic rock quite different in structure and origin
from the surrounding sedimentary strata. On both sides of
the road, between the harbour and the hotel, it is seen
protruding through green patches of verdure in confused
heaps of angular, grey masses. Further notice of this rock is
deferred to a later paragraph dealing with igneous rocks, to
which class it properly belongs.

The bed of limestone previously referred to skirts the
coast in a narrow strip from Balaromin-dubh until it passes
out to sea at Rudha-an-Dobhrain north of Scalasaig. It is
therefore to be seen both north and south of the harbour,
but close to the road it is covered by the granite. A good
exposure of it occurs at the monument. Dark phyllites,
which overlie the limestone, appear at Rudha-dubh and on
the east of Balaromin-dubh, between the outcrop of the limestone and the shore.

Kiloran flags, the strata underlying the limestone, form
most of the hilly land, north and south, from Dun Tealtaig
to Balaromin-dubh. The flanks of the Beannan above the
hotel, and the ridges eastward to Carn-mor, show much bare
rock through a scanty covering of heather and other dark
heathy vegetation often seen on this formation. The
western declivities of Cnoc-na-Faire, on which the monument stands, and the hills of Balaromin show less naked
rock. Associated with the limestone it also encircles Kiloran
Bay, rising into Carnan Eoin, the highest hill. Beinn-a-
Sgoltaire, Beinn-nan-Gudairean, and Cnoc-an-t-Samhlaidh are

others of its most conspicuous eminences. Flags and building-stone have been obtained from it on Beinn-bhuidhe and other places in the neighbourhood of Kiloran, and it has been generally used for building the dry-stone dykes in the vicinity.

The next rock series to appear after passing the houses at Scalasaig are the Milbuie group of phyllites and grits, and the Kilchattan phyllites and sandstones. Deposits of boulder clay at Achadh-Tarsuinn, Learga-mhor, Buailtean-dubha, etc., and alluvium at Leana Laonasaig, Moine Thomach, etc.—the former a product of glacial times, the latter a water-borne sediment of much more recent date—somewhat obscure the rocks close to the road. The phyllites, which follow the Kiloran flags, are abundant in the north-east and north-west of the island, but diminish towards the south, although prominent in Beinn Eibhne. Some of the best hill grazings are on the phyllites, and their paths have been traced through the hills by a greener and more grassy verdure than that on adjoining formations. Binnean-riabhach, Cailleach Uragaig, West Carn-mor, and Beinn-nam-Fitheach are its principal hills, all showing grassy patches to their summits—a feature almost entirely awanting on the flag-stone formations of Carnan Eoin, Beinn-nan-Gudairean, etc. In former times, when churchyards were unprotected, large slabs of this rock, obtained at Mioguras and other places, were used for covering the graves; it is still employed as flags, lintels, and building-stone. The best flags in the island were obtained at Slochd-nam-Bodach, on the east coast, at the junction of the phyllites and epidotic grits.

The white felspathic grits appear over scattered areas in the north-east of the island, and in the Machrins group of grits and mudstones they enter into the formation of part of the hilly land south of Machrins, rising into Carn Chaointe, Carn Bharasaig (at the head of the Glen), Carna-glasa, etc. They protrude through the ground in rounded, hummocky masses, and their light grey colour renders them visible a long way off. Between Machrins and Garvard these features are intensified to such a degree that they give the locality a very rocky aspect. East of Kiloran the grits are marked by a dark brown heathy vegetation, a considerable proportion of which consists of Deer's Hair (Ciob), a species much less common on the adjoining phyllites. The grits are a good building-stone, and have been quarried at Kiloran and Port-mor. They were used in the erection of the recent additions to Colonsay House. The fort - crowned Dun Eibhinn, Carn-na-Cáinnle, etc., are also of this formation. Some curious green-banded grits are to be seen at Milbuie and also near Balanahard, e.g. Beinn Bhreac.

From Moine Thomach to Sguid-Brìdeig we walk over the Kilchattan groups of phyllites (already noticed) and sandstones. On the slopes of Sliabh-riabhach, to the north of the road, the phyllites present a comparatively smooth, verdure-covered surface. The sandstones appear as a band running through the length of the island, north and south, from Beinn-bhreac and the precipice of Geodha-gorm to Balaromin-mor. From Cnoc-an-Ardrigh to Creag-mhor Sguid-Brìdeig they rise into a series of irregular hills and broken rocks. Southwards from Bealach-an-t-Sithean, west of the Slugaidean, they enter into the formation of the bare, stony hills of Carn Fhearguis, etc. Sandstone of the lowest Colonsay series forms the promontory of Ardskenish and the southern half of Oransay as well as the surrounding islets and reefs. Sandstone also appears about Rudha-na-Lice-buidhe in Balanahard.

Between Sguid-Brìdeig and the golf-course lie the Machrins group of mudstones and grits. Mudstones enter into the formation of Beinn Mhuirich as well as of Beinn-nan-Caorach, A' Chrannag, etc., north of Bealach-a-Mhuilinn. Like the Kiloran flags, they show a good deal of rocky surface through a scanty covering of brown heathy vegetation.

South of the road, beyond the boggy ground of Rioma-mhor, alternate beds of mudstones and grits run their length through Garvard to the strand, each kind of rock carrying with it its peculiar characteristics of contour, which are well exposed on both sides of the track from Garvard House to Bealach-an-Aircleich. The mudstones rise up in low weathered escarpments on the east side of the path, the grits presenting their rounded forms on the west. Mudstones reappear in Oransay, rising there into the highest hill, Beinn Orasa. The stone has been much used for building the field dykes about Machrins.

Cutting across the golf-links to the headland of Dun Ghallain, we come to the last of the rock series to be considered—the Dun Ghallain green-banded epidotic grits—which, except for the mudstones and sandstones, are the lowest rocks of the Colonsay series. Near the head of Port Lobh the overlying white felspathic grits are readily distinguished from the Dun Ghallain grits by their different structure. The white grits are not as clearly stratified as the green-banded grits. Dun Ghallain grits curve round the south-west of the island from Turnicil to the head of Traigh-nam-Bàrc, rising there into Carn Spiris, and appearing again in the Cuirn-mhor of Iochdar-na-Garbhaird and on the Oransay side of the strand.

In the north-eastern extremity of the island the relations are more complex. A traverse made from the outcrop of the limestone at Scalasaig to Kiloran Bay passes " first over successively lower beds dipping south-eastwards, and then this dip is reversed and the same series is repeated in ascending order until the Kiloran Bay limestone is once more reached. The anticline thus crossed has a north-easterly trend, and brings to the surface, along its axis, the rocks of the Kiloran and Milbuie groups which underlie the limestone. From the manner in which the limestone circles round Kiloran Bay, it is clear that the latter here occupies the

centre of a synclinal basin. Finally, the northern end
of the island has an anticlinal structure; and a mass of
gneiss, presumably of Lewisian age, occupies the centre of
the fold," *e.g.* to the north of Balanahard Bay and at
Sgeir Nic Fhionnlaidh, etc., "which has a north-easterly
trend." [1]

Igneous Rocks.—Scalasaig granite, already referred to,
is the largest mass of igneous rock in the island. It is a
diorite, and is described by Professor Geikie as a "coarsely
crystalline rock of a very hard, tough, and durable character.
It forms a handsomely marked rock—the pale and dark-
coloured minerals being in about equal proportions—and
might be advantageously employed as an ornamental
building-stone. For structures requiring great strength
hardly a better stone could be desired, as its crushing
power must be very considerable." It was locally used in
the construction of Scalasaig pier. Syenite and kentallenite,
other granitic rocks, appear in Balanahard — the former
above Slochd-a-Chroinn, and the latter in the vicinity of
Cnoc Ormadail. Kentallenite is a particularly interesting
rock, taking its name from Kentallen, where it has been
wrought for years as "the black granite of Ballachulish."
There are four smaller plutonic masses — two in the
northern part of Balanahard, one in Lamalum, and one in
Aoineadh-nam-Muc. Lamprophyre dykes of widely different
ages are numerous in the north of the island, while basalt
dykes (Saor-an-Dao) of Tertiary age are to be met with in
the south.

Glaciation.—Viewed some distance off, the hills of the
island present certain flowing and undulating features which
geologists inform us are characteristic results of glacial

[1] *The Two Earth-Movements of Colonsay,* by W. B. Wright, B.A.,
F.G.S.

action. In glacial times, so we are told, the whole of the country, like the north of Greenland at the present time, was overflowed with ice, which ground and smoothed all the rough surfaces. But the softer rocks, readily affected by the weather, have in the lapse of intervening ages lost much of the rounded outline acquired during the glacial period. Nevertheless, a careful examination will discover well-smoothed and well-striated surfaces. These striæ, which are very well seen on the rocks rising from the strand, were caused by the rubbing of stones as they were pushed along the surface by moving glaciers. They agree in the general direction in which they run—east to west—and this shows that the ice, as might be expected, flowed from the mainland. Here and there, in hollows and on the hill-sides, boulders carried by the ice, differing in structure from the surrounding rocks, are met with. Messrs Wright and Bailey have identified boulders of granite from Glen Fyne, porphyries from Loch Fyne, pebbly sandstones and red conglomerates from an unknown source; also schists, such as those of Jura and Crinan, and other kinds of rocks not entering into the formation of Colonsay. These "erratics," which were carried along by the ice, point to a prolonged movement from the easterly direction.

Boulder clay or till is met with in hollows in various localities. It is usually a reddish coloured, gritty clay, quite unstratified, and abundantly charged with angular and sub-angular stones and boulders, not a few of which show finely striated surfaces. Many of the stones are of local origin, while others come from a distance. The distribution of the boulder clay confirms the supposition regarding the direction from which the ice came. It is generally found in situations sheltered from the full brunt of the ice as it flowed from the mainland. Ant-Allt-ruadh (the Red Burn) has probably derived its name from the discoloration of its waters, in time of flood, by this deposit through which it grooves its channel.

Superficial Deposits.—The principal of these are :—(1) Raised Beach Deposits, (2) Boulder Clay, (3) Peat, (4) Alluvium, and (5) Blown Sands. The most fertile and easily worked soils in the island originated from raised beach deposits laid down at the time when the sea overflowed the land to various levels at and below the 100-feet contour. Though the soils are usually of a light stony nature, they yield good crops. The arable land of Balanahard, Port - an - Tigh - mhoir, East Kiloran, Lower Kilchattan, Machrins, Ardskenish, Garvard, and some other places, as well as Oransay, are of this character. Boulder clay is expensive to work, but with good drainage and tillage yields good crops. The principal areas of it are West Kiloran, Upper Kilchattan, Laon Airidh, West Scalasaig, and Balaromin-dubh. Much of the low-lying land, mostly meadow, such as Kiloran meadows and the low ground bordering Loch Fada—Blar-an-Déabhaidh, Leana-ghlas, etc. —is composed of peat. Unless well looked after in the matter of drainage and top-dressing, grass in these meadows is apt to die out and be replaced by less nutritious plants, such as the Jointed Rush (Frafann), sedges, mosses, and others of a semi-aquatic nature. The principal areas of alluvium to be met with are the low-lying parts of Fang in Kiloran, Leana-na-Cachaleith in Kilchattan, and Moine Thomach in Scalasaig. Tracts of blown sand, irregular and billowy in outline, are to be seen in the north and south ends of the island.

Over most of the hilly land there is a layer of peat, of some depth in the hollows, becoming thin towards the tops of the hills, and frequently allowing bare rock to be exposed on the summits. That the peat layer is gradually increasing in depth may be observed in the peat-cutting areas, where

5

trenches that are made in cutting peat for fuel are seen, in the course of years, to be filling up. When cutting is done, the top spit with the covering vegetation is removed and laid aside; after the available layers of peat have been removed, it is set back in the bottom of the trench. Although the growing process of the peat is noticeable in moist places, it is not so apparent on the dry hill-tops.

Besides those already enumerated, many intermediate grades of soil are to be met with throughout the island— dark, hazel and yellow loams, soils containing a large proportion of humus, and others of a sandy nature, with possibly small areas of calcareous soils in Uragaig and some other places. There is no available record of the soils having been analysed. One of the most fertile loams in the island has been formed by the decay of the " Scalasaig granite." " Much of the fertility of the districts bordering on the sea is derived from shelly sand which the Atlantic supplies more or less abundantly to all the islands of the Inner and Outer Hebrides. This sand supports a beautifully green turf, which in summer time is gay with wild flowers, affording colour effects for which the landscape painter may search the pasture-lands of the mainland in vain. The greater part of Oransay is of this character." [1]

Landscape and scenery are largely dependent on geological structure. Hard rocks resist disintegration and form hills, while the softer and more destructible materials crumble away into hollows and valleys. Every prattling stream that finds its way to the sea assists in the process of landscape sculpture. The running water carves out the hollows and the valleys by cutting and grooving the channels of the streams deeper and ever deeper, carrying away the loosened

[1] " Notes on the Geology of Colonsay and Oransay," by James Geikie, LL. D., F. R. S., F.R.S.E., etc., of H.M. Geological Survey (*Transactions of the Geological Society of Glasgow*, vol. vi. part ii., 1878-79, 1879-80).

material in its downward course. Without considering its
rocky aspect, which possibly strikes the traveller from the
south as nothing short of remarkable, the predominating
note in the island's landscape is the flowing and undulating
outline acquired during the glacial period. It is true,
however, that the softer rocks are yielding to the
disintegrating influence of the weather, and that the
characteristic results of the ice are being slowly but surely
effaced.

Rocks and Flora.—Owing to the identical structure of
Coll, Tiree, and the Outer Hebrides, we would expect to find
their floras very much alike in composition. Such, in fact,
is the case ; but while Mr M'Vicar, in his *Notes on the
Flora of Western Inverness*, classes Tiree with the Outer
Hebrides, he points out that the flora of Coll has many
features in common with that of the schistose islands. In
the actual records of plants there is a greater resemblance
between the floras of the schistose and gneissose islands than
between either of them and those of the basaltic formations.
It should be noted, however, that the soil in many of the
most prolific localities in the former has not been derived
from the rocks of which the islands are composed, but has
been deposited during the raised-beach periods. It is
probably of these raised-beach deposits that much of the
low-lying and most fertile land of the islands—Coll, Tiree,
Barra, etc.—is composed.

A larger number of plants are found in the South Inner
Hebrides than in any of the other groups. The many other
kinds of rocks, besides the schists, entering into the structure of the islands may help to enrich their flora. Certain
calcicole plants are known to occur on the limestone in
Islay, and even in Colonsay, where the area occupied by this
rock is restricted to very narrow limits. The flora of
Lismore is characterised by the common occurrence of

certain species—Wall Rue and Hartstongue Ferns, Rock Rose, etc.—which show a preference for lime.

Plants are found on the basaltic formation which have not been recorded from the South Inner Hebrides. Some species, again, are common to both groups of islands that are wanting in the Outer Hebrides; while a still fewer number are found in the Outer Hebrides and on the basaltic islands that are absent from the South Inner Hebrides.

CHAPTER IV

WOODS, LOCHS, AND PASTURES

Natural Woods.[1]—There are two natural woods—Coille-mhor
and Coille-bheag—on the eastern slopes of the northern half
of the island, and there is reason to believe that formerly
they extended over a much larger area of the island than
they now cover. The woods principally consist of birch of
the Tomentosa section. Varieties of *Betula alba* were discovered, but not the type; investigations in this direction,
however, were not searching. There is a good proportion of
oak (one specimen being identified as *Quercus pedunculata*
and another as *Q. sessiliflora*) in Coille-mhor; and of Aspen
(*Populus tremula*) in Coille-bheag, where some trees 30 to 35
feet high are to be seen. Hazel, Rowan, Willow, Hawthorn,
and Holly also enter into the composition of the woods. A
few good-sized Ash-trees are to be seen in Glaic-an-Uinnsinn,
but it is doubtful if they are truly indigenous. Near the
beginning of last century a path from Colonsay House was
made through Coille-mhor to a summer-house (an Tigh
Còintich) at Cul-Salach, and it is possible that the Ash-
trees were then planted.

Although many of the old Birch-trees are dying out, the
woods are being rejuvenated by young plantations of Birch

[1] This paper on "Natural Woods and Plantations" was read
before the Edinburgh Botanical Society at their meeting on 8th
April 1909.

and Aspen, which are naturally springing up and contending for supremacy with an annual luxuriant growth of bracken. The Woodbine twines over the trees, and festoons along the edges of the numerous rocky gullies that cut up these slopes ; and the Ivy has climbed up and formed pretty evergreens of the more stunted of the forest trees. The Prickly Toothed Buckler Fern grows in profusion, and the little Filmy Fern is also to be seen under mossy banks. White felspathic grits underlie Coille-bheag, and grey phyllites is the principal rock in the vicinity of Coille-mhor, the better condition of the rabbits in the latter being, no doubt, due to the more grassy herbage of the phyllites on which they feed.

Estate Plantations.—The earliest planted trees now to be seen in the island are a few old specimens of Ash and Elm, survivors of a semicircular line of trees which marked the boundary of the original mansion-house garden. These, together with a clump on the southern slope of Beinn-a-Sgoltaire, are believed to have been planted more than a century and a half ago—possibly soon after the first part of the mansion-house had been built, in 1722. In his *Tour* (1772), Pennant remarks on the vigorous growth of the trees around Colonsay House. Other trees within the policies, now grown to a considerable size, were planted about a century ago. The first extensive planting of trees began about eighty to ninety years ago, when Cnoc Càlanda, Pairc Dharaich, Caolachadh, Fail-na-Muc, and Glaic-a-Chuill were, in the course of years, successively planted. A number of smaller plantations, including that at the Manse and Allt-Ruadh in Scalasaig, were planted by Lord Colonsay about fifty years ago.

Such was their tardiness in making headway when planting in the island first began, that it was considered amply satisfactory if the trees grew sufficiently to form good cover. For the first ten years or so they made little progress, and many places had to be planted over and over again. Not until the trees had grown sufficiently to give shelter to one another was the annual growth at all apparent. Protection from animals and shelter from winds were provided at first by dry-stone dykes 5 feet high, extensively built for the purpose. Alder and Sea-Buckthorn were planted along the edges most exposed to the prevailing winds. For wet situations Alder and various species of Poplar were used. Poplars did not last well, and they were also liable to be blown over. Native trees—Birch, Oak, Rowan, etc.—have sprung up in hilly ground where planted trees did not grow.

The most commonly planted of deciduous trees are Ash, Elm, Beech, Sycamore, and Alder, mixed with a lesser number of Lime, Horse-Chestnut, Turkey Oak, White Beam, White Willow, etc. The Ash, though one of the fastest growing and most useful of the trees, is liable to decay. The Beech grows well in dry situations, and has not yet shown any signs of unhealthiness. While most of the trees— Ash, Oak, Conifers, etc.—lose their lower branches in dense shade, those of the Beech have, in many cases, retained their vitality and still produce leaves. This is also the case with the Lime, Chestnut, and perhaps a few other kinds. Of coniferous trees the Larch, Scots Pine, Silver Fir, and Norwegian Spruce have thriven best. The Larch has produced the most valuable timber, but the Silver Firs are the handsomest trees. A few other species—Cluster, Mountain, and Corsican Pines—are also planted. Owing to its tendency to fall over at an early age, the Cluster Pine is often seen with the lower portion of the stem prostrate. Coniferous trees, as a rule, do not take kindly to full exposure to strong winds. *Cupressus macrocarpa* has not been planted as a forest tree, but it appears suitable for the climate. Rhododendrons, which were first planted for cover where the woods were getting thin about thirty years ago, are now thoroughly at home, and every year hundreds of seedlings are spontaneously springing up.

The average annual rate of growth of all the plantations from the time of planting has not exceeded 6 inches. Trees of *Cupressus macrocarpa* and *Acer pseudoplatanus* in good soil and in an exceptionally well-sheltered situation at Kiloran grew at the rate of 1 foot 10 inches per annum for twenty-five years; but that is quite an exceptionally fast rate of growth for this island.

MEASUREMENTS OF SOME OF THE LARGEST TREES IN THE ISLAND.

Kind of Tree.	Age.	Height.	Girth of Stem at 5 ft. from the Ground.	
	years.	ft. in.	ft. in.	
Ash . .	90–100	83 0	5 7	
,, . .	,,	70 0	9 2	
Elm . .	,,	78 0	7 6	
Beech .	,,	74 0	5 10½	
Chestnut .	,,	69 0	4 11	
,, .	,,	60 0	7 3	
Sycamore .	,,	71 6	7 5	
Lime . .	,,	74 0	6 4½	
Alder . .	,,	68 0	5 8	
Larch . .	80–90	71 6	3 2	
,, . .	,,	70 0	4 4	
Scots Pine .	,,	73 0	4 0	
Cluster ,, .	,,	62 6	5 3	
,, ,, .	,,	56 0	8 3	
Norway Spruce	,,	58 0	3 8	
Silver Fir .	,,	67 0	6 7	
Picea Webbiana	...	68 0	5 2	
Douglas Fir .	...	47 0	2 11½	
Spreading Elm	150	50 0	9 0	Spread of branches 90 ft.
Cupressus macrocarpa	54	69 0	11 10	Very short bole; girth taken at 2 ft. from the ground. This tree was grown from seed sent by Colonel (afterwards General) Mitchell from India.

The records from Skerryvore Lighthouse show that these islands are more subject to stormy weather than any other part of the British coast, and the evil effect on the development of trees is manifested by the extremely slow annual rate of growth. The island of Tiree, the land lying nearest to Skerryvore, is destitute of trees. In Colonsay the plantation of Glaic-a-Chuill, which extends well up to the top of Beinn-a-Sgoltaire, provides a striking example of the retarding effects of exposure to winds on the growth of some kinds of trees. The plantation is more than sixty years old, and even in the sheltered hollow at the base of the hill, where the soil is also much better, the trees do not exceed 60 feet in height—an annual growth rate of something less than a foot—while at higher elevations the trees make little or no progress. The following are measurements of four pigmy trees growing near the top of the hill (elevation about 350 feet). They are not taller than the heather among which they grow, but they are still green and living:—Larch (a), height 1 foot 11 inches, girth of stem 2 inches; Larch (b), height 2 feet 2 inches, girth 5½ inches, spread of branches 2 feet 9 inches; Scots Pine, height 1 foot 9 inches, girth 1½ inches; Spruce, height 1 foot 2 inches. In the shelter of the dry-stone dyke close at hand, Spruce and Larch have grown to the height of the dyke but no higher.

The early decay of such trees as the Ash and Elm may sometimes be due to the nature of the ground, as the soil in many places is too shallow to produce heavy timber or to sustain the trees in a healthy, growing condition for long. Often when they are blown over by strong winds the roots lift up all the soil along with them and leave the bare rock exposed. As the result of a moist climate, and one that is detrimental to the health of the trees, we generally find the stems and branches with a luxuriant growth of moss, lichens, etc. Trees with a hard, smooth bark, the Beech in particular, and those that shed their bark, as the Birch, Scots Pine, etc., as well as young trees that are growing rapidly, are sometimes not so much infested with this form of vegetation; but exceptions are not infrequent in every case. *Parmelia perlata*, Nyl., is the commonest of the lichens. *Usnea barbata*, Fr., gives the trees a peculiarly hoary aspect. It is sometimes seen growing on the south-west but not on the north-west side of the trunks. *Sticta pulmonaria*, Ach. (Tree Lungwort) is common on the Ash, Oak, Sycamore, etc. *Pannaria plumbea*, Lightf., and species of *Pertusaria*, etc., are less frequently seen. The following are among the commonest of the mosses found growing on the stems and branches:—*Eurhynchium myosuroides*, Schpr. (on the Birch), *Ulota phyllantha*, Brid. (Ash), *Hypnum cupressiforme*, var. *resupinatum*, Schpr. (White Willow), *Hypnum cupressiforme*, var. *filiforme*, Brid. (Larch), *Metzgeria furcata*, Raddi, and *Brachythecium rutabulum*, Bruch and Schpr.

Ornamental Trees and Shrubs.—The following list may not be without interest as being among those plants that thrive under the influence of the sea air. It should be remarked, however, that all those noted are growing in sheltered situations in Colonsay House grounds near the centre of the island.

Evergreens. — Rhododendrons (*R. ponticum*) thrive in various kinds of soils and situations, and in early summer make a pretty display with a profusion of their purple-violet flowers. The first plants, which were introduced about sixty years ago from Ardlussa in Jura, have developed into large specimens 20 feet high and 40 feet through. Seedlings from the woods were planted by their Majesties King Edward VII. and Queen Alexandra in commemoration of their visit to the island on 29th August 1902. The Holly, though growing naturally in exposed situations, produces berries in any quantity only in sheltered places about Kiloran woods. The Common Laurel (*Prunus lauro-cerasus*) is one of the most valuable evergreens, readily breaking into growth after it is cut back. The Portugal Laurel (*P. lusitanicus*), though beautiful in the young state, has not lasted so well as the

Common Laurel. The Sweet Bay or Bay Laurel (*Laurus nobilis*), from which the laurel wreaths were made by the ancients, also succeeds well. *Escallonia macrantha*, introduced by Messrs Veitch's collector William Lobb from Chili in 1847, has proved a most desirable acquisition to the local list of evergreens, growing into good-sized bushes and forming large expansive hedges. It combines glossy foliage with a profusion, in early spring, of rose-carmine flowers, and a dense habit of growth. Regarded on the mainland as a tender shrub (and here, too, plants have been cut down in severe winters), it is found growing in quantity only in the south-western counties of England, where the flowers are sold to visitors at watering-places. Propagation is readily effected by layers. *Aucuba japonica* (the best evergreen for smoky towns) in its variegated form, Laurustinus (*Viburnum Tinus*), the Holm or Evergreen Oak (*Quercus Ilex*), and Mahonia (*Berberis Aquifolium*) suit the climate. Kinds of Euonymus with variegated leaves make pretty objects in sheltered situations. Cotoneasters do well in exposed positions. *Veronica speciosa*, an attractive evergreen from Van Diemen's Land, bearing numerous spikes of mauve-coloured flowers in the depth of winter, and *V. salicifolia*, now springing up in places spontaneously from seed, are other desirable though old-fashioned subjects. *Aralia* (*Fatsia*) *japonica* has proved hardy in the shrubbery, and its large, glossy leaves make it a valuable evergreen shrub. In 1908 one specimen bloomed profusely, and remained in flower from the end of autumn till the new year. *Desfontainea spinosa*, another of W. Lobb's introductions from Chili (1850), *Chamærops Fortunei*, a Chinese Palm, and a species of *Yucca* which flowered freely in 1907, and is now 12 feet in height with a stem 1½ foot in girth (3 feet from the ground), have been growing out of doors for years. After flowering, the head of the Yucca divided into three shoots.

Deciduous.—The most showy of those introduced include

Lilac, Laburnum, Mock Orange, Weigela, shrubby Spiræas, and Deutzias. The Snowberry spreads rapidly in sheltered places and is suitable for shady situations, and the Flowering Currant (*Ribes sanguineum*) has been found growing spontaneously in the woods. *Fuchsia Riccartoni* grows into large shrubs, but it has been cut down by frost in severe winters. Hydrangeas are a feature, a row on the east side of a Hawthorn hedge near the mansion-house producing in an average season hundreds of huge corymbs of blossom in white, pink, and blue shades. The Lemon - scented Verbena (*Lippia citriodora*) developed stems $3\frac{1}{2}$ inches in diameter and $11\frac{1}{2}$ inches in girth. These measurements are of one of a few stems from the same plant, a seventeen years' growth, killed down to the ground during the severe winter 1894–5.

Conifers look well in the young state, but they do not last. As they increase in height and their heads become exposed to the winds they gradually succumb. For ornamental purposes, *Cupressus Lawsoniana*, raised from seed sent from Vancouver about twenty-eight years ago, has proved the most valuable of the conifers yet introduced. *C. macrocarpa*, from the same source, is developing rapidly into large trees. *Araucaria imbricata* (Monkey Puzzle), *Cedrus Deodara* (Deodor or Indian Cedar), *Pinus excelsa* (Bhotan Pine), *Picea Pindrow*, *P. excelsa* (Common Spruce), and *Juniperus recurva* are among those that have been planted, with more or less satisfactory results during the earlier stages of their growth.

Lochs.—Besides the two principal lochs described below, there are others in the island of smaller size, *e.g.* Loch Colla ($7\frac{1}{2}$ acres), Dubh-loch, Loch-na-Sgùid, Lochan-a-Bhràghad, Loch-a-Raonabuilg, Fionn Loch, Lochan Breac, etc. Most of the lochs have considerable areas of marshy land along their margins. A few years ago, Trout from Loch Fada were placed in Loch-na-Sgùid by a visitor staying at the hotel, and these appear to have multiplied. With the exception perhaps of Eels, the others named are destitute of fish.

Loch Fada, the largest sheet of fresh water in the island, and cutting through about half its breadth almost due east and west, is 1⅘ miles in length, averaging less than $\frac{1}{10}$ mile in width. It is about 124 feet above sea-level, and divided naturally into three divisions, each bearing a local name— Locha-na-Pairce Duibh (east loch), Locha Meadhoin or Locha Gortain Artair (middle loch), and Locha 'n Iar (west loch). The public way is carried over between the east and middle divisions at "an Déabhadh." Although the road was formed there nearly fifty years ago, and much material was carted in at the time and since, to give it a firm bottom, it is still sinking. The out-going stream, which finds its exit into the sea at Kiloran Bay, is from the north side of the east loch. The water is of a more or less brown, peaty nature, and well stocked with Trout. There are considerable stretches of flat, marshy land on the north side, while the southern margin along the base of the hills is frequently rocky. The deepest spot found (about 25 feet) is near Rudha Choilich in the west division : few places, however, exceed 10 feet in depth. Along the shallow margins of both sides of the middle loch the decaying stems and roots of numerous trees are still to be seen. They are locally regarded as species of Bog Oak, but Mr S. Grieve records in addition (see *Proc. Soc. Ant. Scot.*, 1882–3, p. 360) the finding of immense stumps of Goat Willow (*Salix capræa*, L.) along the shores of the loch. Nuts, presumably acorns, were commonly found by persons cutting peat in the neighbourhood.

The three commonest and most conspicuous plants of the lochs are the White Water Lily, Common Reed, and Bottle Sedge, forming, in places, three more or less well-marked zones of vegetation. The Water Lily, during the flowering season in early summer, with its fresh green setting of reeds, makes a pretty display. *Scirpus lacustris* is mostly found on the rocky southern side, while *Cladium Mariscus* is more abundant at the east end. *Litorella uniflora, Juncus bulbosus* (in a variety of shade and form), *Myriophyllum alternifolium, Potentilla palustris, Menyanthes trifoliata,* besides other marsh and aquatic plants, are common along the shallow water and marshy ground at the edges. Beyond the reed zone the water suddenly deepens, and this on more than one occasion has given an unexpected ducking to the unwary juvenile hunter after water-fowls' eggs. This part might well have formed the banks of the original lake, when the water stood much below its present level and the trees whose decaying remains now lie under water reared their leafy heads over dry land.

Callitriche autumnalis, Potamogeton pusillus, etc., driven ashore in windy weather or torn up by water-fowl, indicate to some extent the curious and interesting vegetation that develops under the placid waters of the deeper part of the loch. The plants in the following list were obtained by dragging from the loch boats, and identified, along with those from Loch Sgoltaire, by Mr Arthur Bennett, F.L.S. During dragging operations large masses of *Callitriche autumnalis* and *Potamogeton* several feet in length were brought to the surface.

Callitriche autumnalis.
Potamogeton perfoliatus.
    ,,   *pusillus.*
    ,,   ,, var. *tenuissimus*?
    ,,   *heterophyllus.*
    ,,   *Sturrockii.*
    ,,   *nitens.*
    ,,   *filiformis.*
Elatine hexandra.
Utricularia minor.

Utricularia neglecta.
Naias flexilis.
Myriophyllum alternifolium.
Sparganium minimum.
Juncus supinus, var. *fluitans.*
Litorella uniflora.
Chara fragilis.
    ,,   *vulgaris.*
    ,,   *aspera.*
Nitella opaca.
Ranunculus Drouetii.

The loch lies in an old valley which, at a remote period, had been blocked in on its western end by the throwing up

by the sea of the great shingle bar at Druim Clach,
belonging to the highest of the raised beaches and now
forming the site of several of the most fertile crofts of
Kilchattan. It may be taken for granted, however, that
this did not occur after the submerged trees grew. The
lake must have been already formed when the trees grew
along its margin. The cause of the submergence of the trees
is extremely doubtful. As far as investigations have gone,
there is no evidence to show that they extend more than
a few feet below the surface, and it is possible that the
mere growth of peat at Kiloran might have closed up
the outlet and so submerged them. It is, however, well
to remember that a similar submergence of trees has
been proved in many Norwegian lakes in cases where
the level of the outlet of the lake cannot have changed,
and it is supposed that the forests grew at a time when
the climate was much drier and the level of the lake
consequently lower. Such may have easily been the case
with Loch Fada.

Loch Sgoltaire is a triangular-shaped, islet-studded loch
about 26 acres in extent and lying at an elevation of 200
feet. The name is derived from the Gaelic Sgoilte (cleft),
in reference, doubtless, to the apparent cleavage of the
hills where the loch is situated. Evidently its origin is
totally different from that of Loch Fada, and the hollow in
which its waters now repose may very probably be due to
the scooping power, during glacial times, of the great ice-
sheet that passed westwards over Colonsay from the mainland.
The greatest depth (50–60 feet) is at the narrow apex towards
the north-east end. The bottom is generally rocky, and the
depth becomes less as the loch widens out westward. The
loch has a natural outlet at both ends, the water from the
east or Bealach-a-Mhuilinn end being formerly utilised for
driving a muileann-dubh, while the overflow water from the
west end provides the motive-power for the corn-mill at

Kiloran. The water is pure and good, and the loch forms the source of water-supply for the mansion-house. It is said that the Trout which inhabit it rival in excellence the far-famed Loch Leven Trout.

The, hills surrounding the loch dip rather suddenly down to the water's edge, except at the west end, where there is marshy ground. The margins are usually rocky and stony, with, consequently, an absence of vegetation such as is to be seen in the neighbourhood of Loch Fada. The following plants were obtained by dragging from the boat in the beginning of August, *Callitriche autumnalis* and *Potamogeton heterophyllus* being particularly abundant:—

Potamogeton Sturrockii.	*Nitella translucens.*
,, *perfoliatus.*	*Callitriche autumnalis.*
,, *heterophyllus.*	*Myriophyllum spicatum.*
,, *graminœfolius.*	,, *alternifolium.*
Chara fragilis.	*Litorella uniflora.*

The loch is studded with some small islets—Eilean Beag, Eilean Dubh nam Bò, Eilean Dubh Iain Mhitchel. The largest, which is wooded, is surmounted by the ruins of an old fort, consisting of an inner and an outer work still in a fair state of preservation. Although of some thickness, the walls are but flimsily built of thin flaggy stones. The local tradition that the fort was built by Sir James M'Donald, after his escape from confinement in Edinburgh Castle, is confirmed by Gregory in his *History of the Western Highlands*, page 372, where the following passage occurs:— "About the 18th of June (1615), Sir James arrived at the Isle of Colonsay with several hundred men, and there killed a number of cattle for provisions. While here he built a fort on a small island in a fresh-water loch." The fort had been approached from the northern shore, where the loch is not so deep, by a submerged path in an ingenious manner. Large slabs of stone were piled at intervals on the top of each other in the deeper places; and the defenders, who knew the direction of these steps, were able, with the help of staves, to cross and recross with safety.

Surface vegetation, Loch-a-Raonabuilg, 13th August 1908 :—

(1) A band of White Water Lily surrounds a central oval space of deep water (probably with submerged plants) about $\frac{1}{4}$ acre in area ; (2) a zone of Reeds ; (3) mixed vegetation at the edges, including *Carex inflata, Potentilla palustris, Menyanthes trifoliata, Cladium Mariscus, Mentha aquatica, Juncus acutiflorus, Agrostis alba, Myrica Gale, Sphagnum,* and other mosses.

Carex lasiocarpa is abundant at the margin of Loch-na-Sgüid.

Pastures.—The bulk of the grassy pastures and the arable land lies between sea-level and 250 feet elevation. From 250 to 350 feet (roughly) there is a good deal of bushy sedge and rush-covered ground and areas of heathy moor. Above 350 feet the hills, with the exception of those of phyllite formation, which have grassy patches up to their summits, are clothed with heather. Slopes covered with heather down to the rocky shores are to be seen on the east side of the northern part of the island.

Three well-marked zones of vegetation may again be observed over smaller areas in the hilly pastures : (*a*) heather-covered hill-tops, (*b*) grassy slopes, and (*c*) bushy, often marshy, hollows overgrown with *Juncus acutiflorus*, species of *Carex, Molinia, Agrostis, Erica tetralix, Myrica Gale, Salix,* etc. More frequently the grassy zone is wanting, or is confined to small patches with herbage in varying proportions, according as the ground is well drained or not, of *Festuca ovina, Nardus stricta, Juncus squarrosus, Carex binervis, Carex flacca, Molinia,* etc. The heather in heathy parts is often mixed with *Carex binervis, Scirpus cæspitosus, Molinia, Luzula, Anthoxanthum odoratum,* etc. ;

6

certain species preponderating to a greater degree in certain situations than in others, every hill-side presenting considerable variety in species, and more so in the frequency with which the species occur.

There is reason to believe that grassy pastures, during the last half-century, have decreased in area and deteriorated in quality as regards the composition of the herbage. What within living memory was greensward has now in many places a permanent covering of heather, or is, in summer, adorned with fronds of the ubiquitous bracken. The heather is slowly but surely spreading over the lower hillocks and slopes. Much of the most porous and best-drained land, through which its thick rhizomes can easily penetrate, is overrun by the bracken. The æsthetic value to the landscape of its summer green and its autumn tints is more than outweighed by its debilitating effect on the attenuated herbage underneath.

The herbage in the majority of the pastures, whether well drained or not, has a foundation, often dense, of moss—an undesirable product of a too moist climate. A few fields on the boulder clay have been noticed where this form of vegetation is only present in comparatively small quantities. Animals cannot help grazing it along with the other herbage, but it is avowedly bad for them and difficult to digest. *Hypnum squarrosum*, *Hypnum splendens*, *Barbula ruralis*, are among the common species.

Influence of Sheep on Pastures.—Although it has not been directly proved that sheep have actually exterminated a single species of plant, there is evidence to show that they have to a certain extent upset the balance of nature, and aided in the preponderance of certain kinds over others, the coarsest and least valuable over the finest and most nutritious. With their narrow noses and sharp teeth, sheep nibble the finer grasses and herbage close to the ground, and in the perpetual struggle for supremacy that is silently but constantly going on in the vegetable world, these are gradually being exterminated and replaced by the stronger herbage. It is a matter of common knowledge that the White or Dutch Clover is not nearly so abundant as it used to be. The Heath Vetch, formerly a well-known plant of the hill-sides, is now confined to ledges and other more or less inaccessible situations. Even the hardy Hazel, where it used to be common is represented by but a few scrubby bushes. It may be remarked, however, that although isolated headlands, islets, and other places inaccessible to grazing animals were examined, no species were found which were not seen in other parts of the island.

Mixed stock graze the rough pastures more economically and more evenly than when only one kind of animal is allowed to run over them. Cattle do not eat the herbage as close as sheep, and they eat more of the rough with the fine. Sheep, on the other hand, eat certain plants—Buttercup, Hardhead, Ragwort, etc.—which cattle dislike; and horses, besides showing a partiality to plants which neither cows nor sheep eat, graze the rank herbage on which cattle have left their manure, and which is passed over by cattle themselves. Goats, again, eat many plants and certain lichens (Feusag liath, etc.) which are not touched by other domestic animals.

Common Plants Eaten by Certain Animals Only
(From Withering's *English Botany*)

Spearwort (Glas-leun). Horses eat it; cows, sheep, goats, and swine refuse it.

Corn Spurry (Carran). Horses, sheep, goats, and swine eat it; cows refuse it.

Tormentil (Braonan a' Mhadaidh ruaidh). Cows, sheep, and goats eat it; horses refuse it.

Silverweed (am Brisgean). Horses, cows, goats, and swine eat it; sheep refuse it.

Daisy (Neòinean). Horses, cows, and sheep refuse it.

Colt's-foot (Gallan Greanach). Goats and sheep eat it ; cows are fond of it ; horses refuse it.

Certain plants, *e.g.* seashore and bog plants, cornfield weeds, etc., are confined more or less to certain situations, and need hardly be looked for elsewhere. Some—Louse-wort, Orchis, Bitter Flax, etc.—indicate poor pastures ; others —and these are important for the agriculturist to know, as they can be controlled by drainage—the state of the ground as regards moisture. In dry situations Leguminosæ, Rosaceæ Compositæ, Ericaceæ, Scrophulariaceæ, Plantagineæ, Gramineæ, Filices, etc., are largely represented ; while the prevalence of Ranunculaceæ, Lythraceæ, Umbelliferæ, Polygonaceæ, Juncaceæ, and Cyperaceæ may point to opposite conditions.

COMMON PLANTS INDICATING

WELL-DRAINED SITUATIONS	WET GROUND

High Ground.

Fine-leaved Heath.	Cross-leaved Heath.
Bracken.	Sharp-flowered Jointed Rush.
Fescues.	Sedges.
Wood Rushes.	Common, Spike, Club, and Bog Rushes.
Wild Strawberry.	Bog Pimpernel.
Milkwort.	Bog Starwort.
Sweet Vernal Grass.	Purple Melic-grass.

Low Ground.

Spear Thistle.	Marsh Thistle.
Ragwort.	Bog Ragwort.
Foxglove.	Ragged Robin.
Daisy.	Purple Loosestrife.
Meadow Foxtail.	Marsh Foxtail.
Fine Bent-grass.	Marsh Bent-grass.

Cultivated Ground.

Corn Woundwort.	Marsh Woundwort.
Sow-thistles.	Knotweeds.
Mustards.	Blinks.
Oat-grass.	Bent-grass.
Dead-nettle.	Toad-rush.

THE FLORA[1]

In addition to a numberless host of spore-bearing plants (it is said that there are 40,000 kinds of fungi alone), more than 100,000 species of flowering plants, from all parts of the world, are now known to science. Investigations into regions not previously fully explored are still adding to the number.

Over 2000 species (besides varieties) of flowering plants and vascular cryptogams, grouped into 97 natural orders, are enumerated in the latest (tenth) edition of the *London Catalogue of British Plants*. A careful computation by the writer of plant records, furnished by Mr Arthur Bennett, F.L.S., has resulted in a total of 900 species of flowering plants and vascular cryptogams for the whole of the Western Isles.

The Colonsay list of plants, including Messrs Grieve, Miller, and Somerville's records, now amounts to 580 species and 70 varieties of flowering plants, ferns, and fern-allies. The proportion of varieties to species in the latest edition of the *London Catalogue* is, roughly, 3:5 ; in the local list, 1:8. Without considering a quota of common kinds possibly still overlooked, it is very probable that the island, as a "field" for the critical botanist, is not yet exhausted.

Martin, in the account he gives of Colonsay in his

[1] Read (in part) before the Botanical Society of Edinburgh at their meeting on 10th June 1909.

description of the Western Isles, 1695, mentions that " the middle is rocky and heathy, which in most places is prettily mingled with thick evergreens of *Erica baccifera*, Juniper, and Cat's-tail."

Lightfoot accompanied Pennant to the island in July 1772, and remained on it for several days. In his *Flora Scotica,* which appeared five years later, Lightfoot records six plants (*Carum carui, Convolvulus soldanella, Schlerochloa maritima, Bromus arvensis, Carex arenaria, Triticum junceum*) from Oransay, and four (*Orchis pyramidalis, Gymnadenia albida, Habenaria viridis, Osmunda regalis*) from Colonsay; he having, no doubt, intentionally omitted all the commoner kinds.

The first systematic investigation of the flora of Colonsay was made by Mr Symington Grieve in 1879–81. The results of Mr Grieve's researches are embodied in two interesting papers read before the Edinburgh Botanical Society in April 1880 and in July 1881, and afterwards published in the *Transactions* of the Society, vol. xiv., 1883, pp. 66, 219. About 350 species of flowering plants and vascular crypto-gams, besides mosses, are included in Mr Grieve's lists.

During a brief stay in the island from 3rd to 5th August 1886, Mr W. F. Miller found about 265 species and varieties, most of which had been previously noted. There were some new records for V.C. 102. A short notice with reference to this visit afterwards appeared in the *Journal of Botany*, 1886, p. 308.

While staying at Machrins House in July and August 1906, the late Mr Alexander Somerville, B.Sc., F.L.S., took a keen interest in the local flora. During a prolonged residence in the island the writer had made extensive collections of native plants, which were examined by Mr Somerville, ànd, with new records of his own he was able, before his departure, to raise the list to about 500 species and varieties, including previous collectors' records. The most interesting finds of the season were the Rock Samphire and

the Marsh Helleborine Orchis, then practically two new
additions to the flora of the West of Scotland. A paper by
Mr Somerville on the finding of these plants was afterwards
read before the Edinburgh Field Naturalists' and Microscopical Society, and before the Natural History Society of
Glasgow. His subsequent illness and lamented death
prevented the completion of his intended paper on additions
to the flora of Colonsay. The writer records with gratitude
his indebtedness to the deceased gentleman for much kindly
assistance in the earlier stages of this work : his enthusiasm
for botany, latterly his favourite pursuit, was inspiring.

Local Distribution of Plants.—The particular situations to
which certain plants are confined is not, perhaps, a more
striking feature in their local distribution than the indis-
criminate manner in which others seem to be scattered
throughout the island. Unlike the loftier of the islands,
the elevation (500 feet) is not sufficiently great to affect
perceptibly the distribution of plants, the same species
frequently growing both at sea-level and on the summits
of the hills. Many plants which are affected by exposure
—trees, etc.—are only to be seen in sheltered positions,
more commonly on the eastern half of the island. Others
—Chickweed, Cleavers, Sow-thistle, Herb Robert, Dock,
Silverweed, Stonecrop, etc.—are found growing down to
high-water mark and in various situations inland. Some of
the commonest sea-rock plants—Sea-pink, Sea Plantain, Sea
Spleenwort, and Sea Campion—reappear on rocks near the
centre of the island. Though many species—Willows, Grasses
(*Agrostis alba*, etc.), Sedges (*Carex Goodenowii*, etc.), Amphibious Buckwheat, Dock, etc., seem to be equally well
at home in very marshy and in comparatively dry situations,
the most important factor locally affecting the distribution
of plants, nevertheless, is the condition of the ground as
regards drainage. From the geological formation it is seen

that the crust of the island is formed of hard rock, impermeable to moisture. It is covered with a shallow layer of soil, in many places not more than a few inches in depth. The rain that falls, instead of percolating downwards as it would do if the understratum were pervious, runs along the surface of the rock, or lies in natural basins, forming marshy ground. The water from such situations does not drain away, but is mainly carried off by evaporation—a slow process, resulting in much loss of heat to the ground.

Owing to the proportionately large extent of coast-line in comparison with the inland area, seashore plants form, as might be expected, an important element of the island flora. The northern shore-line, with the exception of Kiloran Bay and the vicinity, is almost wholly rocky, with characteristic sea-rock plants. Salt-marshes, sandy and shingly bays, alternate with rocky promontories round the southern half of the island. Shore pools are frequent on the western shore, and are inhabited by curious plants—species of Tolypella, Ruppia, Chara, Potamogeton, etc.—with a decided preference for brackish water.

Characteristic Plants of the Shore

Plants of the Sea-rocks.—*Ligusticum scoticum, Spergularia rupestris, Crithmum maritimum* (rare), *Beta maritima* (rare). *Asplenium marinum, Sedum roseum, Silene maritima*, and *Statice maritima*, though abundant on the sea-rocks, are occasionally found growing in other situations.

Plants of the Sandy Shore. — *Salsola Kali, Atriplex laciniata, Cakile maritima, Eryngium maritimum* (rare).

Plants of the Salt-marsh.—*Salicornia herbacea, Suœda maritima, Triglochin maritimum, Juncus Gerardi, Scirpus maritimus, Glyceria maritima, Carex vulpina*, etc.

The presence or absence of lime is one of the most important particulars in which petrology affects the distribu-

tion of plants. Though the outcrop of the limestone rock
is restricted to such small areas that, as a factor in plant
distribution, it might be thought hardly worth considering,
yet it is interesting to note that certain alleged lime-loving
plants—*e.g.*, *Carlina vulgaris*, *Orchis pyramidalis*, *Avena
pubescens*, *Thalictrum minus*, *Phyllitis Scolopendrum*, *Anthyl-
lis Vulneraria*—have been found growing in the vicinity.
The neighbourhood is the principal station for *Arabis hirsuta*;
and *Sisymbrium Thalianum*, a plant showing locally a
partiality for old lime-built walls, has also been found here.
Comminuted shells supply to the sandy soil of the districts
bordering the sea an abundance of lime, and provide a
suitable growing medium for such calcicole plants as *Orchis
pyramidalis*, *Gentiana Amarella*, and possibly others of a
lime-loving nature.

The irregular surface of the island, with its great variety
of soils, is such as to provide situations, within a small area,
suitable for many kinds of plants. In the bogs, the con-
sistency of the ground may vary in the compass of a few
square yards from a quaking quagmire to firm peat, each
kind of situation supporting different kinds of plants.
Plants of the Marshy Area (Balanahard bogs)—*Potentilla
palustris*, *Phragmites communis*, *Ranunculus Flammula*,
Menyanthes trifoliata, *Lythrum Salicaria*, *Juncus acutiflorus*,
Agrostis alba, *Carex Goodenowii*, etc. Firmer ground—
Eriophorum angustifolium, *Erica Tetralix*, *Molinia varia*,
Narthecium ossifragum, *Scabiosa Succisa*, *Potentilla erecta*,
Carex flacca, etc.

Plants on Circumscribed Areas growing together

Shingly Shore (Meall-a-Chuilbh, at high-water mark).—
Cnicus lanceolatus, *Sedum anglicum*, *Potentilla Anserina*,
Carex arenaria, *Geranium molle*, *Rumex crispus*, *Plantago
Coronopus*, *Matricaria inodora*, *Geranium Robertianum*.

Cliffs (Dreis-an-t-Sealgair, north shore). — *Ligusticum*

scoticum, Dactylis, Festuca, Lonicera Periclymenum, Rubus, Angelica sylvestris.

Shore Turf (Creagan).—*Carex binervis, C. flacca, Plantago maritima, Statice maritima, Glaux maritima, Cochlearia, Festuca, Lotus corniculatus, Potentilla Anserina.*

Blown Sands (Balanahard Bay). — *Lotus corniculatus, Sedum anglicum, Erodium cicatarium, Veronica Chamædrys, Viola Riviniana, Hieracium Pilosella, Galium verum, Thymus Serpyllum.*

Gaelic Names. — About 200 of the local Gaelic names have been collected, and are here included. Some confusion exists as to the species to which certain names apply. In such cases the names given by the older persons, who had used the plants or known them to have been used for particular purposes, are adhered to. It has not been ascertained with certainty to what plants certain names (Luibh-an-Fhoclain, Lus-na-Miadh, Fionndfhuirneach, etc.) locally refer.

Uses.—In the olden days many of the plants found locally were put to medicinal and other uses; but the generation which so used the plants has gone the way of all flesh, and the information now to be obtained is consequently of a fragmentary nature. Had this work been attempted fifty years ago, it would doubtless have been attended with a much greater measure of success. Such information as could be gleaned from the older inhabitants is noted in the following pages. It may be mentioned here that in the preparation of ointments, etc., the herbs were pounded between stones, as contact with iron or steel was believed to exercise a deleterious effect on the properties of the plants.

EXPLANATORY NOTE

With few exceptions, the nomenclature of the tenth edition of the *London Catalogue of British Plants* has been adhered to. Realising the importance of having a clear distinction between local and general information, care has been taken to precede the date of finding the plant only with local matter; what follows is information collected from various sources, and not referring particularly to the locality. That in connection with orders and genera is of a general character.

The name of the month refers to the time when the plant was found by the writer *in flower*.

Gaelic names in general use but not known to be used locally are enclosed within brackets.

Names, uses, etc., borrowed from Cameron's *Gaelic Names of Plants* are marked C.; those from Withering's *English Botany* are marked W.; and names from Hogan's *Irish and Scottish Gaelic Names of Herbs, Plants, Trees, etc.*, are marked I.

Contractions :—

Ann. = Annual, a plant of one year's duration, *e.g.* Groundsel, Chickweed, Oats, etc.

Bi. = Biennial, a plant of two years' duration, *e.g.* Burdock, Marsh Thistle, Turnip, etc.

Per. = Perennial, a plant of more than two years' duration, *e.g.* Daisy, Bracken, Potato, Willow, etc.

Plants are variable, and, according to their surroundings, some may be annuals while others of the same species are biennials or even perennials.

The vegetable kingdom is divided into two main groups :—

(1) Phanerogams, or flowering plants.
(2) Cryptogams, or flowerless plants.

Cryptogams, which comprise the lower forms of plant life, do not bear manifest flowers nor form seed. They reproduce themselves by spores, hence they are termed spore plants. Ferns (Froineach); Horse-tail (Clo' uisge C.);

Mosses (Còinteach); Liver-worts (Ainean-uisge); Lichens, *e.g.* Ash-coloured Dog-lichen (Cluas-liath an Fhraoich); Tree Lungwort (Crotal Coille); *Parmelia perlata*, Nyl. (Crotal); *Usnea barbata*, Fr. (Feusag-liath); *Xanthoria parietina*, Fr. (Rusg buidhe nan Creag), etc. ; Fungi, including Mushrooms (Bolgag); Moulds (Cloimh liath); Mil-dew (Mil-cheo); Algæ, such as Seaweed (Feamainn) and fresh-water Confervas (Liobhagach-uisge), are all familiar examples of cryptogamic plants. The fungi include a multitude of microscopical kinds (microbes), many being beneficial, while others (disease germs) are hurtful.

Phanerogams bear flowers with stamens and pistils, and usually a perianth consisting of a calyx and corolla. They produce seeds containing an embryo, and are therefore known as seed-plants. Phanerogams embrace the great majority of the best-known plants and the trees. They are divided into two main divisions: (*a*) Angiosperms, comprising practically all the flowering plants; (*b*) Gymnosperms, including the conifers (Pine, Juniper, etc.).

Div. I. *ANGIOSPERMS*

Flowering plants with ovules contained in closed ovaries. They are subdivided into two great classes—Dicotyledons and Monocotyledons.

Class I. DICOTYLEDONS

Dicotyledons include fully three-fourths of our flowering plants, and are easily distinguished from Monocotyledons by their net-veined leaves, and the parts of their flowers being usually in fours or fives. Their stems have a pith in the middle of fibrous or woody tissue, with a separable bark on the outside. Increase in growth takes place by annual additions underneath the bark, seen in the cross-section of a tree by the appearance of concentric circles, or rings, each one marking a year's growth. By counting these circles the age of the tree can be ascertained, and they even indicate the nature of the seasons, whether favourable for growth or not, through which the tree lived. The leaves of Monocotyledons are parallel-veined, and the parts of their flowers arranged in threes; in the stem there is neither a pith in the centre nor a separable bark outside, and they show no annual rings. The embryo has only one seed-leaf; in Dicotyledons there are two—a fundamental distinction. Dicotyledons are further divided into sub-classes, which is beyond the scope of this work to discuss.

RANUNCULACEÆ (the Ranunculus family)

With the exception of the Traveller's Joy, all the British species of the order are herbs. They usually have an acrid or, in some cases, a very poisonous juice, as in the Monkshood (Fuath Mhadaidh, C.), the roots of which have been mistaken for Horse-radish with fatal results. The Hellebore (Elebor, C.) is said to have been used by the ancient Britons for poisoning their arrows. In early summer, such plants of the family as Pæony (Lus a' Phione, C.), Columbine (Lus a' Chalmain), and Larkspur (Sála Fuiseoige, I.) add much to the beauty of gardens. In the depth of winter, the chaste white blossoms of the Christmas Rose unfold. The Wood Anemone (Nead Coille, I.) is recorded from neighbouring islands.

Thalictrum, L.

Perennials, easily recognised by their elegant, maidenhair-fern-like foliage.

T. dunense, Dum.—Meadow Rue. Balaromin-mor, shore rocks.—August.

T. minus, a collinum (Wallr.).—Lesser Meadow Rue.

Rù-beag, C. Rocky banks in Ardskenish Glen. Said to have been locally used for rheumatism; it is therefore sure to have borne a local name.—August.

T. majus, Crantz.—Greater Meadow Rue. Kiloran Bay. —August. One specimen from Kiloran Bay was described by Rev. E. F. Linton as having "broad ovate fruits, near *T. Kochii*."—August.

Ranunculus, L.

Herbs, partial to moist situations, sometimes entirely aquatic. The white Bachelor's Buttons is a double-flowered form of *R. aconitifolius*, a continental species.

R. Drouetii, F. Schultz.—Water Crowfoot. Lion na h-Aibhne, C. Loch Fada.—Per., July.

R. Baudotii c. marinus (Arrh. and Fr.).—Recorded by Mr Somerville.

R. hederaceus, L.—Ivy Crowfoot. Peabar Uisge. Ditches and muddy places. Pounded between stones, it was used as one of the principal ingredients in poultices for king's-evil. —Per., May.

R. sceleratus, L. — Celery-leaved Crowfoot. Torachas Biadhain, C. Port-mor and near Sguid-a-Leanna.—Ann., August. The whole plant is very corrosive, and beggars use it to ulcerate their feet, which they expose in that state to excite compassion. W.

R. Flammula, L.—Lesser Spearwort. Glas-leun. Abundant in marshy situations. Locally used as a substitute for rennet in cheese-making.—Per., July.

R. acris, L.—Meadow Crowfoot; Buttercup. Cearban Feòir. Moist meadows. Leaves, pounded, formed an important ingredient in extracting-plasters.—Per., June.

R. repens, L.—Creeping Crowfoot. Buidheag, C. Sandy ground, Buaile-na-Craoibhe.—Per., July.

R. repens, var. *glabratus*, Lej. and Court.—Kiloran.

R. bulbosus, L.—Bulbous Crowfoot. Fuile Thalmhuinn, C. Garvard, Machrins links, Kiloran Bay, etc.—Per., June.

R. bulbosus, L., var. *parvulus.*—Mossy sand dunes, Kiloran Bay.—June.

R. Ficaria, L.—Lesser Celandine ; Pilewort. (Searraiche.) Gràin-aigein, C. One of the earliest spring flowers to appear, it brightens the landscape with its glossy yellow flowers while many other plants are still dormant. It is abundant in situations that, later on, are overgrown with bracken. The cylindrical tubers of the roots are, in winter, scraped up and eaten by pheasants.—Per., May. Its roots are still used as a cure for piles, corns, etc. C. They were compared to hæmorrhoids, and generally used as a cure for that malady.

Caltha, L.

C. palustris, L.—Marsh Marigold. (Lus Buidhe Bealltainn.) Common in wet situations.—Per., April.

Trollius, L.

T. europæus, L. — Globeflower. Leolaicheann (?), C. Recorded by Mr Miller.

Aquilegia, L.

A., var.—Columbine. (Lus a' Chalmain.) Kiloran woods, on the ledge of a low precipice.—Per., June.

BERBERIDACEÆ (the Barberry family)

A small order, mostly herbs and shrubs. Evergreen species (Mahonia) are ornamental and hardy, thriving locally.

Berberis, L.

B. vulgaris, L. — Barberry. (Geàrr - Dhearc. Preas Deilgneach.) Introduced, and now growing naturally in a few places in Kiloran. The roots were sometimes boiled and drunk for jaundice.—June. A yellow dye is obtained from the root. The berries are acid and astringent, and sometimes preserved.

NYMPHÆACEÆ (the Water Lily family)

Aquatic plants of great beauty. *Victoria regia,* the Queen of Water Lilies, from the Amazon regions, produces leaves measuring 12 feet across. The Sacred Bean of the Egyptians (*Nelumbium speciosum*) is closely allied.

Castalia, Salisb.

C. alba, Wood. — White Water Lily. Ruaimleadh. Common in the lochs. A black dye, for dyeing wool and yarn, is obtained from the large roots, which are cut up and boiled.—June.

PAPAVERACEÆ (the Poppy family)

Annuals, abounding in milky juice and remarkable for their narcotic properties. Some kinds, such as the Shirley Poppies, produce flowers of exquisite beauty.

Papaver, L.

P. somniferum, L.—Opium Poppy. (Codalan; Lus a' Chadail.) North side of Port-mor.—August. The opium of commerce is the dried juice of this species, obtained by incising the poppy-heads before they are ripe. Asia Minor, Egypt, Persia, and India yield the principal supply of the drug.

P. dubium, L. — Smooth-headed Poppy. Bollasgan. Cultivated fields.—June.

P. Argemone, L. — Pale or Prickly-headed Poppy. Recorded by Mr Grieve.

7

FUMARIACEÆ (the Fumitory family)

Delicate herbs; *Dielytra spectabilis* from China is one of the best-known garden representatives of the order, thriving locally.

Fumaria, L.

F. Bastardi, Bor.—Garden weed, Kiloran. Confirmed by Mr H. W. Pugsley.—Ann., October.

F. officinalis, L.—Fumitory. Lus Deathach Thalmhuinn, C. Common in dry fields.—Ann., July.

CRUCIFERÆ (the Crucifer family)

Plants of the order are easily recognised by their cruciform-shaped flowers, the four petals forming a Maltese cross. None are poisonous; many, such as the Watercress, have pungent juices; while others possess antiscorbutic properties. Under cultivation their juices become milder, and the various organs, as in the Cabbage (Càl), Turnip (Neup), Cauliflower (Càl Gruidhean, C.), Radish (Raidis), etc., tend to become succulent. Oil of rape, gold of pleasure oil, etc., are obtained from the seed. Woad (Buidhe Mor, I.) dyes blue, and was used by the ancient Britons for staining their skin. Stock, Wallflower (Lus-leth-an-t-Samh-raidh), Alyssum, Candytuft, Rocket, Honesty, etc., are popular garden ornaments.

Radicula, Hill

R. Nasturtium - aquaticum, Rendle and Britten. — Common Watercress. Biolair. Abundant in running water. Used as salad; it was also prepared like cabbage—boiled, pounded, and seasoned—and used in broth (brot biolarach).— Per., July.

Barbarea, Br.

B. vulgaris, Ait.—Yellow Rocket. Roadside, Kiloran, and manse garden - wall; rare. — Bi., June. In Sweden the leaves are used in salads early in spring and late in autumn; also boiled as kale. W.

B. verna, Aschers. — American Cress. Garden wall. Cultivated in gardens as a salad.—Bi., June.

Arabis, L.

A. hirsuta, Scop.—Hairy Rockcress. New Cave.—Bi., June.

Cardamine, L.

C. pratensis, L.—Lady's Smock; Cuckoo-flower. Lus-an-Fhògair (?) Flur na Cubhaig, C. Common at the sides of ditches. Known by the younger people as Peabar-uisge. —Per., May.

C. hirsuta, L.—Hairy Bittercress. Roadsides, Kiloran.— Ann., May.

C. flexuosa, With.—Kiloran woods; local.—Bi. or Per., June.

Draba, L.

D. incana, L.—Twisted-podded Whitlow-grass. Recorded by Mr Grieve.

Erophila, DC.

E. verna, E. Meyer.—Whitlow-grass. Biolradh Gruagáin (?), I. A tiny plant, one of the earliest to flower in spring. Common on sandy ground near the shore.—Ann., April.

E. praecox, DC.—East side of Traigh-nam-Bàrc. A small specimen found on the rocky hillocks at Cròisebrig, Balanahard, resembled, in Mr Bennett's opinion, the sub-species *E. inflata*, Wats.—May.

Cochlearia, L.

A few species, including the Horse-radish (Ràcadal) so much cultivated in gardens as a condiment.

C. officinalis, L.—Scurvy-grass. Am Maraiche. Biolair Creige, W. Dun Ghallain rocks.— Bi. or Per., June. Well known for its antiscorbutic properties.

C. danica, L.—Recorded by Mr Miller.—Ann. or Bi.

C. grœnlandica, L.—Biolair Tragha, I. Common on the shore turf.—July.

Sisymbrium, L.

S. Thalianum, Gay.—A few localities, on old walls and in the vicinity of the limestone rock. (*Arabis Thaliana*, A. B.).—Ann., May.

S. officinale, Scop.—Hedge Mustard. Fineul Mhuire, I. Recorded by Messrs Miller and Somerville.—Ann. or Bi.

Camelina, Crantz

C. sativa, Crantz, *b fœtida* (Fr.).—Fetid Gold of Pleasure. Rare.

Brassica, L.

Cabbage, Cauliflower, Broccoli, Kale (Càl Broilein), Kohlrabi, etc., originated from *B. oleracea*, a British native, on record from Islay.

B. Napus, L.—Rape, or Cole-seed. Meacan Raibhe, I. Cultivated field.—Ann. or Bi., July. Grown in this country as green fodder, and on the Continent for the seed, from which the oil of rape is expressed.

B. Rapa, L.—Common Turnip. Neup. Vacant ground. —Ann. or Bi., June. The culture of turnip (improved kinds) as a field crop is believed to have been introduced by Sir Richard Weston, on his return to England from Flanders in 1645.

B. nigra, Koch.—Black Mustard. Cornfield.—Ann., June. The mustard of commerce is usually prepared from the seeds of this variety and of *B. alba.* The former is chiefly cultivated in Lincolnshire and Yorkshire, and the latter in Essex and Cambridgeshire.

B. arvensis, O. Kuntze. — Charlock ; Wild Mustard. Sgeallan. A too common cornfield weed. In the young state it was prepared and eaten like cabbage. — Ann., August.

B. Erucastrum, Vill.—Vacant ground. Introduced with feeding stuffs.—August.

Capsella, Medic.

C. Bursa-pastoris, Medic.—Shepherd's Purse. Luibh-a-Sporain. Sporan Buachaille, W. Well-known garden weed. —Ann., May. The young radical leaves were brought to market to Philadelphia and sold for greens in the spring of the year. (Barton.) W.

Lepidium, L.

L. ruderale, L.—Narrow-leaved Cress. Vacant ground, Kiloran.—Ann., August.

L. sativum, L. — Garden Cress. Biolair Frangach, I. Rubbish-heap, Kiloran.—Ann., June. A supposed native of Persia, and cultivated in this country since the middle of the sixteenth century.

Thlaspi, L.

T. arvense, L.—Field Pennycress. Praiseach Féidh, C. Vacant ground, Kiloran.—Ann., July.

Cakile, Mill

C. maritima, Scop. — Sea Rocket. Fearsaideag, C. Kiloran Bay sands.—Ann., August.

Raphanus, L.

Garden kinds of Radish are varieties of *R. sativus*, L.

R. Raphanistrum, L.—Wild Radish ; Jointed or White Charlock. Meacan Ruadh, C. Cultivated field, Kiloran.— Ann., July.

VIOLACEÆ (the Violet family)

Without considering the many beautiful pansies now in cultivation, the Sweet Violet alone would raise this order in the estimation of all lovers of flowers.

Viola, L.

V. palustris, L.—Marsh Violet. Badan Measgan (?), I. Marshy ground.—Per., June.

V. odorata, L.—Sweet Violet. (Fail-Chuach.) Introduced.—Per., May. Its roots are said to be purgative.

V. Riviniana, Reichb. — Dog Violet. Sail - Chuach. Dail Chuach, C. Known by the younger people as Broga Cuthaig, a name applied by older persons to the Harebell.— Per., May. Beneficial in skin-diseases.

V. Rivinana × *sylvestris*.—East of Bruach-mhor.

V. tricolor, L. — Pansy Violet ; Heartsease. Spòg-na-Cuthaig, C. Abundant in sandy fields.—Ann., July. The numerous forms of pansies now in cultivation have been obtained by selection from this species, and by hybridising it with *V. grandiflora*, *V. altaica*, etc. Goirmín Searradh, I.

V. arvensis, Murr.—Field Pansy. Cultivated fields.— Ann., July.

V. Curtisii, Forster.—Sandy hollow east of Traigh-nam-Bàrc.—Per., August.

V. Curtisii, Forster, *f. mackaii.* — Blown sands, Port Easdail.

V. lutea, Huds.—Yellow Mountain Violet. Recorded by Mr Grieve.—Per.

POLYGALACEÆ (the Milkwort family)

A small order with bitter and astringent qualities, and a milky juice in the root. The American Snake Root is used for chronic bronchitis and asthma, and was a reputed antidote against the poison of snakes.

Polygala, Linn.

P. vulgaris, L.—Common Milkwort. Lus - a' - Bhainne. Recorded by Mr Miller.—Per.

P. serpyllacea, Weihe.—Siabunn-nam-Ban-Slth. Common on dry heaths and pastures. When rubbed between the hands a lather is formed, hence the local name.—Per. June.

CAROPHYLLACEÆ (the Pink family)

The British species of the order are numerous, and easily recognised by their general habit, swollen nodes, and opposite leaves. They are generally found in dry situations. Many, as the Soapwort (Lus-an-t-Siabuinn), are pervaded by a saponaceous principle, but they are usually devoid of active properties. The various species of Dianthus—Carnations, Pinks, Sweet-William, etc.—alone would raise this family to a position of no mean ornamental value.

Silene, L.

Certain species of this numerous genus are known as Catchflies, from the fact that they are coated with sticky hairs to which small kinds of flies and other insects adhere.

S. maritima, With.—Sea Campion. Sea-rocks, northern shore. Although one of the showiest of our earliest summer flowers, no local name has been discovered for it.—Per., June.

S. noctiflora, L.—Night-flowering Catchfly. A cornfield weed. Recorded by Mr Grieve.

S. dichotoma.—Vacant ground, Kiloran. An alien that

is becoming naturalised in many parts of the country.—
August.

Lychnis, L.

L. alba, Mill.—White Lychnis. Roadside, Scalasaig.—Bi.
or Per., July.

L. dioica, L.—Red Campion. Lus-a-Ròs. Círean Coileach, I. Shady roadsides.—Per., July.

L. Flos-cuculi, L.—Ragged Robin. Caorag-Leana, C.
Frequently adorning wet meadows.—Per., June.

L. Githago, Scop.—Corn Cockle. Iothros, C. A cornfield weed of sandy places.—Ann., July.

Cerastium, L.

One of the best-known garden representatives of the genus
is *C. tomentosum* (Snow-in-Summer), much used for edgings
and carpet-bedding.

C. tetrandrum, Curt.—Common, and, near the shore, often
with grains of sand adhering to the stems and leaves.—Ann.,
July.

C. viscosum, L.—Broad-leaved Mouse-ear. Garden weed.
—Ann., June.

C. vulgatum, L.—Mouse-ear Chickweed. Cluas Luchag.
Frequent in dry situations.—Per., June.

Stellaria, L.

Usually found growing, locally, in moister places than the
members of the preceding group.

S. media, Vill.—Common Chickweed. Fliodh. One of
the commonest weeds.—Ann., July. It follows the British
settler to all parts of the globe.

S. Holostea, L.—Greater Stitchwort. Tùirseach, C.
Glasaird, rare.—Per., June.

S. uliginosa, Murr.—Bog Starwort. Ditches and wet
places.—Ann. or per., June.

Arenaria, L.

A. serpyllifolia, L.—Thyme-leaved Sandwort. Not uncommon on sandy ground near the sea.—Ann., August.

A. peploides, L.—Sea-Purslane. Kiloran Bay sands.—Per., June.

A. peploides, var. *oblongifolia.*—Sands, Port-an-Tigh-mhoir. June.

Sagina, L.

Small, tufted, inconspicuous herbs.

S. maritima, Don.—Sea Pearlwort. Port-mor, south side. —Ann., September.

S. apetala, Ard.—Lawns and pastures.—Ann., June.

S. procumbens, L.—Procumbent Pearlwort. As this species is said to have been one of the plants that were formerly fixed over doors for good luck, it probably had a local name. —Per., July.

S. procumbens, L., sub. sp. *confertior,* Norman.—Scalasaig, shore.

S. subulata, Presl.—Top of Carnan Eoin.—Per., July.

S. nodosa, Fenzl.—Knotted Spurry. Moist situations, Kiloran.—Per., August.

Spergula, L.

S. arvensis, L.—Corn Spurry. Carran. (Cluain Lìn.) Common weed of cultivated fields.—Ann., July. It was formerly grown as a forage plant, the knowledge of its culture having been brought from Holland about 1740. Experience shows it to be very nutritious to cattle that eat it; poultry are fond of the seed; and the inhabitants of Finland and Norway make bread of it when their crops of corn fail. W.

Spergularia, Presl.

S. rubra, Pers.—Common Sand-Spurry. Sandy ground, Cul-Salach and Poll Gorm. Pure white flowers.—Ann. or Bi., July.

S. salina, Presl.—Recorded by Messrs Miller and Somerville.

S. salina, c. neglecta (Syme).—Shore rocks, Port-mor.—Ann. or Bi., June.

S. marginata, Kittel.—Salt-marsh, Port-an-Obain, Scalasaig.—Per., August.

S. rupestris, Lebel,—Rocks, Lamalum.—Per., June.

PORTULACEÆ (the Purslane family)

More or less succulent herbs. Purslane (Purpaidh), from South America, is grown for salads.

Montia, L.

M. fontana, L.—Blinks; Water Chickweed. Shady woods and moist places.—Ann. or Bi., May.

M. fontana, a minor, All.—Ditch, Port Sgibinis.

ELATINACEÆ (the Elatine family)

A small order of one European genus.

Elatine, L.

E. hexandra, DC.—Water Pepper. West Loch Fada.—Ann., July.

HYPERICACEÆ (the Hypericum family)

Confined in Britain to the following genus—herbaceous and shrubby perennials with opposite undivided leaves, often dotted with minute oil-glands. *H. calycinum* (Rose of Sharon, Aaron's Beard), from South-East Europe, is often planted in gardens, being useful for shady situations.

Hypericum, L.

H. androsæmum, L.—Sweet Amber; Tutsan. Caora-caothaich. The globular, shining fruit was credited, if eaten, with inducing madness; hence the local name.—July.

H. perforatum, L.—St John's Wort. Eala Bhuidhe, W. Recorded by Mr Grieve. Used in medicine. Badge of Clan M'Kinnon.

H. quadrangulum, L.—Square-stalked St John's Wort. Beachnuadh Firionn, C. Frequent by ditch-sides.—August.

H. humifusum, L.—Trailing St John's Wort. Upper side of Buaile Sheagail.—August.

H. pulchrum, L.—Small, upright St John's Wort. Luibh Chaluim Chille. Common ou dry, heather-clad hills. The local name is now frequently, but incorrectly, given to the Bog Asphodel.—July.

H. elodes, L.—Marsh St John's Wort. Abundant in peat-bogs.—August.

MALVACEÆ (the Mallow family)

Though only sparingly represented in Britain, this is an important tropical order, many of the species furnishing useful fibre from the inner layers of the bark. There is a remarkable absence of noxious qualities. The order includes some wonderful tropical species. Cotton (Cotan) is obtained from the hair-like appendages that clothe the seeds of various species of Gossypium. Hollyhock (Ròs Mall) and Malope are handsome for the flower-garden. The Tree Mallow, a British species, grows in exposed situations near the sea.

Malva, L.

M. moschata, L.—Musk Mallow. One plant in pasture, Druim-an-Déabhaidh, where it is known to have been growing for many years.—Per., July.

M. sylvestris, L.—Common Mallow. Ucas Fiadhain, C. Recorded from Oransay by Mr Grieve, and the only species in this list not known to occur also in Colonsay.

Tiliaceæ (the Lime family)

A large tropical order, yielding valuable fibre. "Jute" is obtained from Indian species, and is largely used in the manufacture of carpets and other fabrics. The wood of the lime is easily worked, and the best in this country for carving.

Tilia, L.

T. vulgaris, Hayne.—Lime-tree; Linden. (Crann Teile.) Introduced. — June. The inner bark furnishes "Russia matting."

Linaceæ (the Flax family)

A small order of herbs and shrubs characterised by the tough fibre of the inner bark.

Radiola, Hill.

R. linoides, Roth.—Allseed. Bare and stony sides of paths.—A minute annual; July.

Linum, L.

A large genus, some species—annuals and perennials—with showy but short-lived flowers, in various colours.

L. catharticum, L.—Purging Flax. Caolach Miosa. Lionnam-Ban-Sìth. Common in barren heaths and pastures. Locally used for its cathartic properties.—Ann., August.

L. usitatissimum, L.—Common Flax; Linseed. Lion. At one time largely cultivated for its fibre; used locally in the manufacture of linen.—Ann., June. The seed is valuable for the oil it contains, and is largely used medicinally and for feeding stock.

Geraniaceæ (the Geranium family)

Particularly numerous in South-West Africa, they are chiefly remarkable for the beauty of their flowers. Some

species are easily recognised by their characteristic "pea-flowers"; the fruit is commonly a pod, more or less resembling that of the pea or bean. The properties of the order are most varied; some, as Peas (Peasair), Beans (Pònair), Lentils (Gráin-Fheileóg, I.), etc., being valuable food-plants, others (Liquorice = Maide-milis) are medicinal, not a few being poisonous. Other species furnish valuable wood, fibres, dyes (Indigo = Guirmein), gums, resins, oils, tan, etc. Clover, Vetch, Lucerne, Sainfoin (Coirm Coilig, I.) are cultivated as forage plants. The little swellings commonly seen on the roots of leguminous plants are inhabited by "bacteroids" which have the power of drawing on the free nitrogen of the air and passing it on to the plant, with the result that the ground is often richer in nitrogen after a leguminous crop than it was before. In the tropics, the order is represented by gorgeous flowering trees, which, after the flowering period, produce pods several feet in length. Crab's-eyes, Circassian Beads, and other tropical seeds are pretty, and strung by the natives into necklaces and various ornaments. Laburnums (Bealaidh Frangach, I.) and some species of Broom and Genista thrive near the sea and are highly ornamental. Lupins (Searbhán Faolchon, I.) are among the handsomest of early summer-flowering herbaceous plants.

Ulex, L.

U. europœus, L. — Whin, Furze, or Gorse. Conasg; Beala'ach. Abundant in places. A green dye is obtained from the bark. The young growths are eaten by cattle, and during the flowering period the plant is reputed to give a rich yellow colour to butter.—March. Sometimes sown as a forage plant on the mainland (at the rate of 20 to 30 lbs. per acre). It was cultivated for this purpose in England as early as 1725, and a century previous to that in Wales. The tops are crushed before giving them to cattle.

Cytisus, L.

C. scoparius, Link.—Broom. Bealaidh. Recorded by Mr Miller. Within living memory two plants existed : one on an uncultivated hillock in Caolachadh, and one in Glaic-a-Chuill. Like the whin, it yields a green dye.

Ononis, L.

O. repens, L.—Rest or Wrest Harrow. Sreang Bogha, C. Sandy ground, Kiloran Bay.—Per., August. The rootstock creeps underground, and is sufficiently tough to obstruct agricultural implements during tilling operations ; hence the common English name.

Medicago, L.

A genus of useful forage plants. Purple Medick or Lucerne is suitable for sowing in light, sandy soils, its roots penetrating the subsoil sometimes to the depth of 10 to 12 feet. It is not so much cultivated in Scotland.

M. sp.—Specimens found at the edge of a field in Machrins did not arrive at sufficient maturity to be certain whether they were *M. sylvestris*, Fr., or *M. falcata*, L.—August.

M. lupulina, L.—Black Medick ; Nonsuch. Common in the vicinity of cultivated fields. — Ann. or Bi., June. Although the produce is bulky, cattle are not very fond of it, and only eat it with seeming relish when mixed up with more nutritious and esteemed food.

Trifolium, L.

T. pratense, L.—Red or Purple Clover. Seamrag Dhearg. Sùgag, C. In Kilchattan, where it used to thrive most luxuriantly as a forage crop and give several cuttings in the season, it will now hardly grow, the ground probably having become what is termed "clover sick."—Bi. or Per.,

July. Its culture was introduced to England from Flanders by Sir Richard Weston in 1645, but it was not cultivated in Scotland till 1720–30.

T. medium, L.—Zigzag or Meadow Clover. Interstices in rocks, Baile-Mhaide.—Per., July.

T. hybridum, L.—Alsike Clover. Garden weed. Kiloran. —Per., August. It is one of the best of perennial clovers, and it has been found to thrive in soils which are termed by farmers "clover sick."

T. repens, L.—White or Dutch Clover. Seamrag Gheal. Common. The finding of the four-leaved Clover (Seamragnam-Buadh) was regarded as a sign of good luck.—Per., June. It is now used as the national emblem of Ireland, although believed to be a plant of comparatively recent introduction to that country. *Oxalis acetosella*, the Common Wood Sorrel, is said to have been the original "shamrock." "An indispensable ingredient of pastures, but where it is too prevalent it has a tendency to scour the cattle which graze on it."

T. procumbens, L.—Hop Trefoil. Pasture, Kiloran.— Ann., July.

T. dubium, Sibth.—Small Yellow Trefoil. Seangan, C. Uncultivated hillocks, Lower Kilchattan.—Ann., June.

Anthyllis, L.

A. Vulneraria, L. — Kidney Vetch; Lady's - fingers. Meòir Mhuire; Cas-an-Uain, C. Common on dry, uncultivated hillocks and rocky places.—Per., July. It was celebrated from early times as a plant that was efficacious in the cure of wounds.

Lotus, L.

L. corniculatus, L.—Bird's-foot Trefoil. Blathan-buidhenam-Bò. Abundant in dry situations. It is said to impart a good yellow colour to butter.—Per., July. It is eaten with avidity by cattle, and owing to the depth to which it sends its roots into the ground it remains green when other plants are burnt up by drought.

L. uliginosus, Schkuhr.—A much larger plant in all its parts than the preceding, and common in moist situations.— Per., August.

Astragalus, L.

A. danicus, Retz.—Recorded by Mr Grieve.—Per.

Vicia, L.

V. hirsuta, Gray.—Hairy Tare. Peasair Luchag. Lower Kilchattan ; locally regarded as indicating poor soils.—Ann., July.

V. Cracca, L.—Tufted Vetch. Caornan. Hedges, and borders of fields.—Per., July.

V. sepium, L.—Bush Vetch. Peasair-nan-Each. Road-sides ; frequent.—Per., June.

V. sativa, L.—Common Vetch. Peasair Capuill. Corn-fields.—Ann., August.

V. angustifolia, L.—Narrow-leaved Vetch. Recorded by Mr Somerville.—Ann.

V. lathyroides, L.—Spring Vetch. Only seen on Cnoc Eibriginn.—Ann., May.

Lathyrus, L.

L. pratensis, L.—Meadow Pea. Peasair Bhuidhe, C. Common in moist places.—Per., July.

L. sylvestris, L.—Everlasting Pea. Recorded by Mr Grieve.—Per.

L. montanus, Bernh. — Heath Vetch ; Heath Pea. Corra-Meille. The tuberous roots were dug up and eaten raw, or tied in bundles and hung up to the kitchen roof to dry, and afterwards roasted. Used for flavouring whisky. The wooden trowel for digging up the roots was called "pleadhag." A plant with stringy roots, occasionally dug up by mistake, was known as Corra-Meille Capuill. —Per., July.

ROSACEÆ (the Rose family).

The order includes the best of our hardy fruits—Apple (Ubhal), Pear (Peur), Plum (Plumbas), Peach (Pietseog, I.), Cherry (Sirist), Strawberry, and Raspberry. Other species— Spiræas, Roses, etc.—are characterised by the beauty and the fragrance of their blossom. The seeds of the drupaceous fruits—Plum—yield the highly poisonous prussic acid.

Prunus, L.

The only British genus with a stone fruit, including the Bullace (Bulastair, C.), Damson (Daimsin, C.), Gean (Geanais, C.), Wild Cherry (Craobh Shirist), and Bird Cherry (Craobh Fhiodag, C.). *P. persica*, a supposed native of Persia or China, is the parent of the many delicious varieties of Peach and Nectarine (Neochdair, C.) now to be obtained. Other fruit belonging to this genus are the Apricot (Prúine Airméineach, I.), from Central Asia; Prunes (Plumbais Seargtha, I.), the fruit of a species of plum dried in heated ovens, largely in France; Sweet Almonds (Cnò-Almoin), the kernels of the fruit, from North Africa and South Europe. Almond oil is expressed from Bitter Almonds. The Common Laurel (*P. lauro-cerasus*) and the Portugal Laurel (*P. lusitanicus*) are among our most useful evergreens.

P. spinosa, L.—Blackthorn; Sloe. Sgitheach Dubh; Draighionn-Dubh. Near sandy shores it forms low, almost unimpenetrable thickets. Sloes (Airneag) are now rarely produced.—April. In Ireland, one of the favourite woods for the "shillelah."

Spiræa, L.

S. Ulmaria, L.—Meadow-sweet; Queen of the Meadows. Luibh - a - Chneas. (Lus - Cneas - Chuchulainn). Banks of ditches and moist meadows. Used in dyeing.—Per., July.

Rubus, L.

A large genus, comprising in Britain some two hundred kinds of brambles alone. The Cloudberry (Oidhreag), a miniature bramble without prickles, occurs on the Scottish mountains. The following were identified by the Rev. W. Moyle Rogers, F.L.S. They were collected from the east and north-east half of the island when it was well on in September, rather too late in the season for easy identification.

R. idæus, Linn.—Raspberry. Suth-Craobh. Now well established in Kiloran woods.—July.

(?) *R. Rogersii*, Linton.—Specimens not sufficiently good to be named with certainty.

R. plicatus, Wh. and N.—Moist, peaty ground. Ceann Locha.

R. rhamnifolius, Wh. and N.—Rocky ground near the shore, Slochd-na-Sgarbh.

R. dumnoniensis, Bab.—Rocky ground, Slochd-nam-Bodach. Mr M'Vicar found this one of the commonest Brambles in Mull, Lismore, and various places on the mainland.

R. pulcherrimus, Neum.—Bramble; Blackberry. Dreas-na-Smeur; Smeuran. One of the commonest kinds in the island. An orange dye was obtained from the roots. The leaves were applied to burns. Fruit much esteemed in jam and jelly making.

R. Selmeri, Lindeb.—Fairly common about Kiloran.

R. pubescens, Weihe. — Clais-na-Faochag; rather common. "A very luxuriant form, nearer to my variety *subinermis*, Rogers, than to the type" (Rev. W. M. R.).

R. pubescens-subinermis, f. — "I am greatly interested

in the —*pubescens-subinermis* form, as it is not only the only example that I have seen from Scotland, but it also is not strictly identical with either our type or variety." Hillocks, Scalasaig meadows, on the " Scalasaig granite."

R. macrophyllus, Wh. and N., *b Schlechtendalii* (Weihe). —Open situation, Kiloran woods.

R. dumetorum, Wh. and N.— One of the commonest roadside brambles. Rev. W. Moyle Rogers wrote with regard to a number of specimens submitted : " All, or nearly all, one and the same form apparently, but hardly agreeing well with any of our named varieties."

R. corylifolius, Sm.—Recorded by Mr Miller.

R. cæsius, Linn.—Dewberry. Preas-nan-gorm-Dhearc, C. Growing in a heap of stones, seaside, Slochd-dubh-Mhic-a-Phi.

R. saxatilis L.—Stone Bramble. (Caora-bada-Miann.) Recorded by Mr Somerville.

Geum, L.

G. urbanum, L.—Common Avens ; Herb Bennet. (Machall Coille.) Northern slopes of Beinn-nan-Gùdairean.—**Per.**, August At one time used in medicine.

G. rivale, L.—Water Avens. (Machall Uisge.) Damp gullies below Uragaig.—**Per.**, July. The root-stocks of all these are powerfully astringent, and also yield a yellow dye. **C.**

Fragaria, L.

F. vesca, L.—Wild Strawberry. Suth-Làir. Abundant on dry slopes on the eastern half of the island. The fruits are gathered by children.—**Per.**, May.

Potentilla, L.

P. norvegica, L. — Vacant ground, Kiloran, — **Ann.**, August. An alien, now spreading in the country.

P. sterilis, Garcke.—Barren Strawberry. Ledges of rocks, Tigh Iain Daraich.—**Per.**, May.

P. erecta, Hampe.—Tormentil. Braonan a' Mhadadh ruaidh. Abundant in heaths and moors. The roots were boiled and strained, and the juice given, in milk, to calves as an astringent. It was also given to human beings.—Per., July. Roots dye red. W. It is generally used for tanning their nets by fishermen in the Western Isles, who call it "Cairt-Lair." C.

P. reptans, L.—Creeping Cinquefoil. (A' Chòig-bhileach.) Edge of pool, Cul-Salach ; rare.—Per., August.

P. Anserina, L.—Silverweed. Brisgean. Bàrr Bhrisgean, C. Growing at the seaside down to high-water mark. The roots were gathered and eaten raw and also boiled like potatoes. The local value, in former times, attached to this as an article of food may be realised from the fact that it was termed "an seachdamh aran" (the seventh bread).—Per., July.

P. palustris, Scop. — Marsh Cinquefoil. Còig-bhileach Uisge ; Cnò Leana, C. Abundant in marshes.—Per., June.

Alchemilla, L.

A. arvensis, Scop.—Parsley Piert. Spíonán Mhuire, I. Common in dry situations.—Ann., July. It was formerly eaten raw or pickled. W.

A. vulgaris, L., *b alpestris*, Pohl.—Lady's Mantle. Dearna Cridhe. Copan an Driuchd, C. Pastures.—Per., July. Owing to its astringent properties it is said to be fatal to cows if they eat it in large quantities. W. A decoction from the plant was believed to have the effect of restoring faded beauty, and an application of the dew from the leaves was credited with similarly happy results.

Rosa, L.

It is but fitting that the hybridiser should not have spared his best efforts in procuring adequate representatives of this, the queen of flowers, and the emblem of the "predominant partner" in the Empire. From a comparatively small number of species the **3000** or so of varieties now in cultivation have been produced. These are, for convenience, grouped into many classes — Tea Scented, Hybrid Teas, Hybrid Perpetuals, Climbing, Ramblers, Chinese, Ayrshire, etc. They are of all sizes, from the miniature fairy roses, less than 1 foot in height, to strong climbers which send out shoots 12 feet long, and more, each season. There are singles and doubles in almost every conceivable shade of colour. Otto or attar of roses—the finest perfume prepared —is obtained, by distillation, from the petals of various sweet-scented kinds. As a political emblem—*e.g.* the Red Rose of the House of Lancaster, the White Rose of the House of York, etc.—the Rose is historical. The best of our garden varieties are budded on to the Briar or some other hardy kinds. The following, collected in the north-eastern end of the island (in September mostly), were kindly named by Mr W. Barclay, Perth.

R. spinosissima, L.—Burnet or Scottish Rose. Dreas-nam-Mucag. Dry slopes and banks. A fine brown dye (with copperas) is obtained from the plant.—June. The Scottish Roses have originated from this species.

R. spinosissima, f. — Sheltered situation, Glasaird. Specimens of this, which were at first thought to be the var. *Ripartii*, Déségl, have been described by Mr Barclay as "a variation which differs from the type in having glandular peduncles, teeth of the leaves irregular, many simple teeth, but with a good many having a toothlet attached, which sometimes bears a gland. I do not think it has been specially named. Var. *Ripartii* has composite glandular teeth, and besides has the midrib and veins of the underside of the leaves more or less glandular, which is not the case with the specimens submitted."—June.

R. tomentosa, Sm.—Rudha-na-Coille-bige ; not uncommon. "The *tomentosa* forms do not differ very much from each other; they seem to belong to the same group of variations."

R. Eglanteria, Huds.—Sweet Briar. Dreas Chùbhraidh. Kiloran woods.—September. This species is frequently planted for the fragrance of its leaves.

R. Eglanteria, b comosa (Rip.).—Caolachadh wood.

R. canina, L., *a lutetiana* (Léman).—Dog-rose. Earra-Dhreas. Port-a-Bhuailtein; common. Mucag-fhailm = hip of rose.—September. The leaves of every species of Rose, but especially of this, are recommended as a substitute for tea, when dried and infused in boiling water. W.

R. canina, L., *g dumalis* (Bechst.).—Rocky ground, Claise-na-Faochag.

R. glauca, Vill.—Caolachadh wood. Mr Barclay remarks of the somewhat scanty material submitted for examination: "Seems to be a *glauca* form, but not well characterised. No. 2 apparently the same, but even more distant from the type."

R. coriifolia, Fr., var.—Wood, Ceann Locha. "The rose you send is a var. of R. *coriifolia*, Fr., with very glaucous, hairy leaflets, composite glandular toothing, somewhat glandular on the midrib, and with a gland here and there on the secondary veins; peduncles and backs of the sepals glandular, and with broadly oval or somewhat obovate fruits, also more or less glandular. It does not really correspond with any named variety known to me, but may be considered as somewhat intermediate between *Watsoni* (Baker) and *Bakeri* (Déségl)" (W. B.).

Pyrus, L.

Shrubs and trees with showy flowers. From the Crab Apple (Craobh Ubhal Fhiadhain) the innumerable varieties now in cultivation have sprung. The best kinds in this country are grafted on to the Crab or Paradise stocks—the former for large, the latter for dwarf trees. For general cultivation the Apple is the most profitable of all our fruits.

The varieties which have sprung from the Wild Pear (Craobh Pheur Fhiadhain) are hardly less numerous than in the case of the Apple. The Quince (Cuinnse), Medlar (Meidil), Service (Cheòrais, C.), etc., bear edible fruit.

P. Aria, Ehrh.—Introduced. Kiloran woods.—May.

P. Aucuparia, Ehrh.—Rowan ; Mountain Ash. Caora-Caorthainn ; Caorthann. One of our prettiest native trees, adorned in early summer with cymes of white blossom and later with clusters of scarlet fruit.—June. Any part of the tree was regarded in some parts of the Highlands as a sovereign charm against enchantment and witchcraft. C.

P. Malus, L.—Apple-tree. Craobh Ubhal. One tree growing naturally among whin bushes near Bealach-a-Mhadaidh.—June.

Cratœgus L.

C. Oxyacantha, L.—Hawthorn ; May. Draighionn (geal). Often seen in the vicinity of ruins. Used for hedges. Sgeachag = Haw (fruit).—May. Cultivated forms, in various shades from white to scarlet, are numerous.

SAXIFRAGACEÆ (the Saxifrage family)

Exotic genera include shrubs and trees, of which Hydrangea, Escallonia, Deutzia, Mock Orange, are familiar garden examples, thriving locally.

Saxifraga, L.

The varieties are numerous, and useful for rockeries, also suitable for shady situations. "Highland" species are to be found on the higher mountains of the northern isles.

S. umbrosa, L.—London Pride. (Càl Phàruig.) Introduced.—Per., June. A Continental plant which, by long cultivation, has become established in this country.

S. tridactylites, L. — Rue-leaved Saxifrage; Rock-foil. Rocky hills at Poll Gorm and Cròisebrig near the shore. One of the tiniest of local plants.—Ann. or Bi., May.

S. hypnoides, L.—Mossy Saxifrage. Locality uncertain. —Per.

Chrysosplenium, L.

C. oppositifolium, L.—Golden Saxifrage. (Lus-nan-Laogh.) Gloiris, I. In early summer it carpets the woods, in moist, shaded situations, with its golden blossom.—Per., May.

Parnassia, L.

P. palustris, L.—Grass of Parnassus. Fionnan Geal; Fionnsgoth, C. Moist ground near the seashore in Garvard, the Glen, etc.—Per., July.

Ribes, L.

R. Grossularia, L.—The Gooseberry. Gròiseid. Kiloran woods, to which the seeds were carried from neighbouring gardens by birds.—May.

R. rubrum, L.—Red Currant. Dearcan Dearg. Kiloran plantations. The White Currant (Dearcan Geal) is only a form of this species, and red and white fruit are sometimes to be seen on the same bush.—April.

R. nigrum, L.—Black Currant. Dearcan Dubh. Among Whins, Cnoc Reamhar-mor, and plantations, Kiloran.—April.

CRASSULACEÆ (the Crassula family)

Xerophytic plants, with crowded, succulent leaves, often growing in rocky or sandy situations. Various kinds of Sedum, House Leek (Lus-nan-Cluas, C.), Navelwort (Làmhainn Cat Leacain), etc., are commonly grown in gardens, their neat habit and slow growth making them suitable for edgings and carpet-bedding designs.

Sedum, L.

S. roseum, Scop.—Roseroot. (Lus-nan-Laoch.) Clefts and ledges of the sea-rocks of the northern shore.—Per., May. The root, which furnishes an astringent, has the fragrance of a rose, particularly when dried. W. The badge of the Clan Gunn.

S. anglicum, Huds.—Stonecrop. Garbhan Creige. Abundant. Pounded together with groundsel, it was used to reduce swellings, particularly on horses.—Per., July. It was formerly eaten as a salad, and considered a delicacy. C. Locally also known by the younger people as Biadh Seangain; Biadh-an-t-Sionnaich.

S. acre, L.—Wall Pepper; Biting Stonecrop. Grafan-nan-Clach, C. Not uncommon in sandy and rocky situations round the shores.—Per., June.

DROSERACEÆ (the Sundew family)

A small order, confined in Britain to the following genus.

Drosera, L.

Insectivorous plants (perennials) obtaining their nitrogen from the bodies of insects which they assimilate. The upper surface of the leaves is clothed with curious viscid hairs, each terminated by a small gland. These glands secrete a sticky fluid, to which small insects that are attracted to the plants adhere. The irritation set up by their struggles to free themselves causes the leaves to close up, effectively imprisoning their tiny victims. After they are assimilated, the leaves, often encumbered with skeletons of those already digested, open out to entrap more insects.

D. rotundifolia, L.—Sundew. Lus-na-Fèarnaich. Abundant in peat-bogs.—July. The whole plant is acrid, and sufficiently caustic to erode the skin; but some ladies mix the juice with milk so as to make it an innocent and safe application to remove freckles and sunburns. W.

D. anglica, Huds.—Long-leaved sundew. Bogs near Loch Colla ; rare.—July.

D. longifolia, L. — Marshy ground, Rioma-mhor, Machrins.—August.

HALORAGACEÆ (The Mare's-tail family)

Principally aquatic herbs. *Hippuris vulgaris* (Mare's-tail) has been recorded from Tiree and the Outer Hebrides.

Myriophyllum, L.

M. spicatum, L.—Water Milfoil. East Loch Fada and Loch Sgoltaire.—Per., August.

M. alterniflorum, DC. — Whorled Milfoil. Snàthainn Bhàthadh, C. A much commoner plant than the preceding ; at the edge of the lochs and in burns.—Per., July.

Callitriche, L.

C. stagnalis, Scop.—Water Starwort. Biolair-ioc. Abundant in shallow waters. Formerly used as an ingredient in plasters for promoting suppuration.—Per., June.

C. intermedia, Hoffm.—Slow-flowing burn, Kiloran.—June. (*C. hamulata*, Kuetz.—A. B.)

C. autumnalis, L.—Autumnal Starwort. Common in the deeper water of the lochs.—July.

LYTHRACEÆ (the Loosestrife family)

The few British representatives of the order are herbs. Some exotic species are valuable for their timber ; others furnish fruit, dyes, etc. The pomegranate (Gràn-Abhal) is mentioned in Deuteronomy as one of the products of Palestine.

Peplis, L.

P. Portula, L.—Water Purslane. Ditch, roadside between Machrins and Scalasaig. Not uncommon.—Ann., July.

Lythrum, L.

L. Salicaria, L.—Purple Loosestrife. Creachdach. Lusna-sith-Chainnt, C. Abundant in wet situations.—Per., August.

ONAGRACEÆ (the Œnothera family)

Fuchsias from Chili are familiar garden representatives of the order.

Epilobium, L.

E. angustifolium, L.—French Willow; Rose Bay. Seilachan Frangach, C. Introduced, and now spreading in sheltered situations in Kiloran.—Per., August.

E. parviflorum, Schreb.—Hoary Willow-herb. Damp situation, Balanahard.—Per., September.

E. montanum, L.—Broad Willow-herb. An Seilachan, C. Crevices in rocks, Balaromin-mor.—Per., July.

E. obscurum, Schreb.—Ditch, Kiloran; common in wet situations.—Per., July.

E. palustre, L.—Marsh Willow-herb. Marshy places.— Per., July.

Circœa, L.

C. lutetiana, L.—Enchanter's Nightshade. Fuinnseach, C. Growing among rolled stones, seaside, Uragaig. Local.— Per., August.

C. alpina, L.—Recorded by Mr Miller.

UMBELLIFERÆ (the Umbellate family)

One of the largest British orders, herbs, generally easily recognised by their deeply divided leaves and flowers arranged in umbels. In this great group there are few of decorative value, but some—Celery (Seilere, I.), Carrot (Curran), Parsnip (Curran Geal), Skirrets (Brislean)—are (or were) valued as esculents, and others—Parsley (Fionnas Gàraidh), Fennel (Lus-an-t-Saoidh), Angelica (Lus-nam Buadh), Anise (Anis; Ainis Cùbhraidh, I.), Coriander (Lus-a-Choire), Dill (Dile; Lus Min, I.), Chervil (Costag-a'-Bhaile Gheamhraidh), Alexanders (Lus nan Gràn Dubh)—are grown as pot-herbs, and for garnishing, medicine, etc. Hemlock, Fool's Parsley, Dropwort, and others have poisonous properties.

Hydrocotyle, L.

H. vulgaris, L. — Marsh Pennywort. Lus-na-Peighinn. Oibheall Uisge, I. Forming part of the bottom herbage in wet situations.—Per., July. It is said to be injurious to sheep, producing white rot.

Eryngium, L.

E. maritimum, L.—Sea Holly. Cuilionn Tràghadh. One specimen seen growing at the edge of the blown sands, Dunan Easdail. It was gradually eaten up by sheep, and did not flower.—Per. The roots are sometimes preserved in sugar and eaten as a sweetmeat.

Sanicula, L.

S. europœa, L.—Wood Sanicle. (Bodan Coille.) Abundant in Kiloran woods, and also seen in Coille Bheag.—Per., June. In former times it possessed a high reputation for healing wounds.

Conium, L.

C. maculatum, L.—Hemlock. (Minmhear.) A highly poisonous biennial. Balaromin-mor and Lower Kilchattan. —July. Used in medicine as a sedative and antispasmodic.

Apium, L.

Occupants generally of marshy situations. *A. graveolens*, L., is the Wild Celery (Lus na Smalaig, C.), a native of sea-coast districts of England and Wales.

A. nodiflorum, Reichb. fil.—Procumbent Marshwort. In streams where they enter into the sea at Kiloran Bay and Port Sgibinis.—Per., July.

A. inundatum, Reichb. fil.—Least Marshwort. Fualactar, C. Slow-flowing ·part of Abhuinn-a-Ghlinne.—Per., June. (*Helosciadium inundatum*, A. B.)

Carum, L.

(?) *C. Carvi*, L.—Caraway. Carbhaidh. In the neighbour-hood of old gardens. The so-called seeds (carpels) were used for flavouring oat-cakes.—July.

Ægopodium, L.

A. Podagraria, L.—Goutweed; Bishopweed. (Lus-an-Easbuig.) A troublesome garden weed.—Per., July.

Pimpinella, L.

A numerous genus, including *P. anisum*, the fruit (Aniseed) of which is aromatic and carminative and largely employed in medicine.

P. Saxifraga, L.—Burnet Saxifrage. Roadside, Kiloran; rare.—Per., July.

Conopodium, Koch.

C. majus, Loret.—Earthnut; Pignut. Braonan Coille. Abundant in well-drained situations in the north-east of the island. The globular root-tuber was dug up and eaten by children.—Per., June.

Myrrhis, Scop.

M. Odorata, Scop.—Sweet Cicely. (Cos Uisge.) Dry situations in Kiloran woods and Ardskenish Glen.—Per., July.

Anthriscus, Bernh.

The genus includes *A. Cerefolium* (Chervil), which is cultivated as a pot-herb.

A. sylvestris, Hoffm.—Wild Chervil. A weed of waste places, recorded by Messrs Grieve and Somerville.—Bi.

Crithmum, L.

C. maritimum, L. —Sea Samphire. Saimbhir, C. Seen in one place on the rocky shore. Recorded by Mr Somerville in 1906.—Per., July. It has recently been discovered in the Outer Hebrides. Samphire is much sought after for pickling, sometimes at the risk of human life (men being suspended from the rocks by ropes), though other plants procured at less hazard, as Salicornia and Aster, are frequently substituted. W. It is cultivated as a salad and for seasoning.

Œnanthe, L.

Œ. Lachenalii, C. Gmel. —Parsley Dropwort. Edge of shore pools south of Port-mor.—Per., July.

Œ. crocata, L.—Hemlock Water Dropwort. Aiteodha. Abundant on the banks of streams and in wet gullies at the shore. Used in poultices. The green leaves are often eaten with impunity by cattle in the summer time, but the roots are poisonous. A number of years since, eight stirks died after eating the roots which had been thrown out of a ditch when cleaning it in the winter time.—Per., July.

Ligusticum, L.

L. scoticum, L.—Scottish Lovage. (Siunas.) Plentiful in the rocks of Meall-a-Chuilbh with a northern exposure.—

Per., July. The root is reckoned a carminative, and an infusion of the leaves in whey is good physic for calves. It is, besides, used as a food, eaten raw as a salad or boiled as greens. Pennant's *Tour*, 1772.

Angelica, L.

A small genus, including *A. Archangelica* (Garden Angelica), a native of the Continent, and long cultivated for confectionery.

A. sylvestris, L.—Wild Angelica. Geobhastan. Woods and moist situations. Children make "squirting-guns" out of the hollow stems. The flowering umbel was locally known as Bollachdan. In the winter time rabbits burrow into the ground and eat the root-stock.—Per., July.

Peucedanum, L.

P. sativum is the common Parsnip (Curran Geal), a native of the south of England, and the parent of the present cultivated forms.

(?) *P. Ostruthium*, Koch.—Masterwort. (Mòr Fhliodh.) Kiloran.—Per., July.

Heracleum, L.

H. Sphondylium, L.—Hogweed; Cow-parsnip. Giuran. Common in well-drained situations, and cut in the green state for cattle.—Per., July.

Daucus, L.

D. Carota, L.—Wild Carrot. Curran Talmhainn. Abundant in rather dry situations.—Bi., June. The various forms of Garden Carrots (Currain-bhuidhe) have been produced from this species.

ARALIACEÆ (the Aralia family)

A large order of woody-stemmed plants, represented in Europe by the following species only. *A. japonica* from

9

Japan is a desirable addition locally to the list of evergreen shrubs. "Rice-paper" is cut out of the pith of *Aralia* (*Fatsia*) *papyrifera*, a tree of Formosa.

Hedera, L.

H. Helix, L.—Ivy. Eidheann ; Duchas. Uillean, C. Often growing in exposed situations against perpendicular rocks ; hence the saying with the double meaning, "Theid an duchas an aghaidh nan creag." The leaves were sown into a cap for covering children's heads which were breaking out into sores—a complaint now practically unknown locally among infants. Planted against their walls, it helps to dry damp houses.—October. Many "gold" and "silver" variegated forms are in cultivation. The badge of the Gordons.

CAPRIFOLIACEÆ (the Honeysuckle family)

Mostly shrubs, some of them possessing purgative and emetic properties. Laurustinus, a pretty evergreen, and the Snowberry, a deciduous North American shrub with large white berries, are useful plants for shrubberies. Seedlings of the latter were found in crevices on a garden wall. The Guelder Rose (Céiriocan, C.) and the Wayfaring-tree (Craobh Fhiadhain, C.) are British natives. The Danewort (Fliodh-a'-Bhalla, C.) was formerly credited with many healing qualities.

Sambucus, L.

S. nigra, L.—Common Elder. Droman. Frequently planted as a boundary hedge around cottage gardens. The inner bark was largely used along with other herbs in the preparation of healing ointments for burns, etc. Boys aspiring to be pipers made chanters of the young branches, which are full of soft pith and easily bored.—June.

Lonicera, L.

L. *Periclymenum,* L.—Honeysuckle ; Woodbine. Caora Mhèa(ng)lain. Twining round trees, over ledges of rocks, etc. Berries were eaten by children.—July.

RUBIACEÆ (the Peruvian Bark family)

A very large and important tropical order, including the Coffee plant. Quinine is extracted from the bark of various South American species of Cinchona (Peruvian Bark). The root of a shrubby Brazilian plant finds its way into commerce under the name of Ipecacuanha. The Dyer's Madder (Madar) is largely cultivated for its scarlet dye. Some species—Gardenia, Ixora, etc., are fragrant and pretty evergreen stove-plants.

Galium, L.

G. *verum,* L.—Lady's Bedstraw. Ruin ; Ruamh, C. Dry banks and rocky ledges.—Per., August. The roots are said to yield a red dye, and the plant to have been used in making rennet in some parts of the Highlands.

G. *saxatile,* L.—Heath Bedstraw. Madar Fraoich, C. Abundant in open heaths.—Per., June.

G. *palustre,* L., *c Witheringii* (Sm.).—Marsh Bedstraw. Common in marshes and ditches.—Per., July.

G. *uliginosum,* L.—Recorded by Messrs Grieve and Miller.

G. *Aparine,* L.—Goosegrass ; Cleavers. Seircean Suir'ich ; Luibh-na-Cabhrach. Neglected places. Used locally as a strainer in the preparation of flummery.—Ann., July. The branches are used by the Swedes instead of a sieve to strain milk ; young geese are very fond of them. W.

Asperula, L.

A. *odorata,* L.—Woodruff. Lus-na-Caithimh, C. Noted by Mr Somerville, probably an introduced plant. When drying it gives off a sweet scent, and was formerly used for imparting an agreeable odour to clean linen.

Sherardia, L.

S. arvensis, L.—Field Madder.   Balla Cnis Chu Chulloin, I.   Not rare in well-drained situations, Kiloran.—Ann. or Bi., May.

VALERIANACEÆ (the Valerian family)

Annual herbs and herbaceous perennials, often aromatic or strong scented.   Spikenard (Spiocnard), long valued in India as a perfume, is an aromatic oil obtained from the root of a Himalayan species.   The roots of the Great Valerian (An Tribhileach) are grown in England for medical use.

Valeriana, L.

V. sambucifolia, Mikan.—Cat's Valerian ; All-heal.   Ard-skenish Glen ; local.—Per., July.

Valerianella, Hill

V. olitoria, Poll.—Cornsalad ; Lamb's Lettuce.   Leitis Luain, I.   A small annual, common on the sand-dunes.— May.   Cultivated in places as a salad plant.

DIPSACEÆ (the Teasel family)

Herbs or undershrubs.   The dried flower-heads of the Fuller's Teasel (Liodan-an-Fhùcadair, C.) is used for raising nap on cloth.

Scabiosa, L.

S. Succisa, L. — Blue Scabious ; Devil's-bit.   Gille-guirmein.   Abundant.   White forms seen.—Per., August. The dried leaves are used to dye wool yellow or green. (Linn.)   The plant furnishes a familiar example of the præmorse or bitten-off root.   This gave rise to the superstitious belief that "the divell, for the envie he beareth to mankind, bitt it off, because it would otherwise be good for many uses." W.

> "Gille-, Gille-guirmein
> Mu'n teid thu mu'n cuairt
> Buailidh mi mo dhòrn ort"

was rhymed (locally) by children as they held the unoffending flower in the left hand with the right closed in a threatening attitude over it. The stalk was surreptitiously twisted beforehand, and held in such a way as to allow the flower-head to revolve only at will.

S. arvensis, L.—Field Scabious. Recorded by Messrs Grieve & Miller.

COMPOSITÆ (the Composite family)

This is the largest order of flowering plants, comprising over 10,000 species. British representatives are easily recognised by their inflorescence ; the flowers are collected into dense heads surrounded by an involucre, the whole resembling a single flower, as the Daisy, Dandelion, etc. Bitterness is their prevailing characteristic ; some—Wormwood (Burmaid), Southernwood (Meath Challtuinn ; Surabhan, C.), Camomile (Camabhil) — possessing, in addition, aromatic secretions. The milky juice of Lettuce (Liatus, C.) has narcotic properties. Sunflower seeds yield oil. Another species of Sunflower, Jerusalem Artichoke (a native of Brazil), furnishes edible tubers. The Globe Artichoke (Farusgag) is grown for its succulent, immature flower-heads. The blanched stems of Cardoons and the roots of Salsafy and Scorzonera are used as vegetables. Endive (Eanach Gàraidh) is blanched for salad. The roots of Chicory (Castearbhain), roasted and ground, are used (a not unwholesome addition) to adulterate coffee. To the gardener the ornamental species—Sunflowers (Grian-bhlath, I.), Chrysanthemums, Asters, Dahlias, Everlastings, etc.—belonging to this group are, for decorative purposes, indispensable.

Eupatorium, L.

E. cannabinum, L.—Hemp Agrimony. Cainb Uisge, C. Bank of stream, Ardskenish Glen.—Per., September. This is the only British representative of a large genus containing about 400 species, chiefly American.

Solidago, L.

S. Virgaurea, L.—Golden Rod. An t-Slat-Oir. Common on dry, rocky hills about Uragaig.—Per., August.

Bellis, L.

B. perennis, L.—Common Daisy. Neòinean. Meadows and pastures. One of the principal ingredients used in the preparation of healing ointments. The leaves, and sometimes the upper portion of the root-stock, are eaten by rabbits in winter time, but all animals avoid it when they can.— Per. Flowering nearly always.

Aster, L.

The species of the genus are numerous in North America, some of which — Michaelmas Daisies — are popular late autumn flowering plants.

A. Tripolium, L.—Sea Aster. Eoinean Sàilean. Marine turf, strand side.—Per., September.

Antennaria, Gaertn.

A. dioica, Gaertn. — Mountain Everlasting. Not uncommon, usually in dry situations.—Per., May.

Gnaphalium, L.

G. uliginosum, L.—Marsh Cudweed. Cnàmh Lus; Luibh n-Chait, C. Roadsides, Kiloran.—Ann., August.

G. sylvaticum, L.—Wood Cudweed. Sandy fields, east Kiloran.—Per., August.

Inula, L.

I. Helenium, L.—Elecampane. Aillean. Old disused garden, Glasaird. Formerly cultivated for its medicinal properties.—Per., July. Its root is credited as being tonic, diuretic, and diaphoretic. The plant is said to have been named by the Romans after the Fair Helen of Troy.

Bidens, L.

B. tripartita, L.—Bur-Marigold. Ditches, Kiloran and Leana-na-Cachaleith.—Ann., September.

Achillea, L.

A. Millefolium, L.—Milfoil; Yarrow. Cathair Thalmhainn. (Lus-Chosgadh-na-Fola.) Abundant in sandy fields and pastures.—Per., July. It is highly astringent. Recommended for sowing in dry sheep-pastures, but more as a condiment than for affording direct nutritive matter.

A. Ptarmica, L.—Sneezewort. Meacan-Ragaim ; Lus-a-Chorrain, C. Common in moist situations on the low ground.—Per., July.

Anthemis, L.

The true Camomile (*A. nobilis*) is cultivated for its flowers, long used as a stimulating tonic.

A. Cotula, L.—Stink Mayweed. Fineul Madra, I. Vacant ground, Kiloran.—Ann., August. This and others of the tribe were popular cures for swellings and inflammation. C.

A. arvensis, L.—Camomile. Camabhil. Frequent in the vicinity of old habitations. An infusion of the leaves and flowers was drunk for strengthening the stomach. Also boiled in milk for a similar purpose. Used as an ingredient in poultices for promoting suppuration.—Per., July.

Chrysanthemum, L.

For late autumn flowering and winter decoration the numerous forms now in cultivation are unequalled. *C. sinense,* a native of China introduced into this country in 1764, is the parent of many of our large flowered kinds.

C. segetum, L. — Corn Marigold. Dithean. A showy weed of cultivated fields.—Ann., July. It was used to soothe throbbing pains.

C. Leucanthemum, L.—Ox-eye Daisy. Neòinean Mor. Edges of fields, Kiloran. — Per., July. This plant was esteemed an excellent remedy for king's-evil. C.

Matricaria, L.

M. inodora, L.—Corn Mayweed. Buidheag-an-Arbhair, C. Common in waste places and at the seashore.—Ann., July.

M. inodora, b salina, Bab.—Shingly shore, Creagan; leaves succulent.—September.

M. maritima, L. — Sea rocks, Druim - na - Faoileann. Locally rare, and on record only from one vice-county.— September.

M. Chamomilla, L.—Wild Camomile. Recorded by Mr Grieve.

Tanacetum, L.

T. vulgare, L. — Tansy. Lus - na - Fraing. Grown in cottage gardens for flavouring purposes.—Per., September.

Artemisia, L.

Aromatic herbs or shrubs. The Common Wormwood (Burmaid) and the Sea Wormwood are British natives with aromatic and intensely bitter properties. The Roman Wormwood and Tarragon (from Siberia) are grown as pot-herbs. All are species of Artemisia.

A. vulgaris, L.—Mugwort. Liath Lus. On the raised-beach deposits. The leaves were smoked by old people.—Per., August.

Tussilago, L.

T. Farfara, L.—Coltsfoot. Gallan Greanach. An infusion of the leaves was drunk for whooping-cough. A popular remedy for chest troubles. The leaves were smoked as a substitute for tobacco.—Per., April.

Petasites, Hill

P. ovatus, Hill.—Butterbur. Gallan Mor. Kilchattan. The leaves, which are larger than those of any other British plant, were used as sunshades by children when playing.— Per., April.

Senecio, L.

This is the largest genus of the order, occurring in all parts of the globe. Some species, of horticultural value, have recently been introduced from China.

S. vulgaris, L.—Groundsel. Grunnasg. Common garden weed. It was used as an ingredient in the healing ointments. Also applied to prevent suppuration.—Ann. Nearly always in flower. Plants from the blown sands described by Mr Bennett as being " near the variety *integrifolius*, Opiz."

S. sylvaticus, L.—Mountain Groundsel. Recorded by Mr Miller.—Ann.

S. Jacobœa, L.—Ragwort. Ballan Buidhe. Abundant in dry pastures. Ballan Buidhe Boirionn, the first year's growth or a barren form of the Ragwort, was commonly used as an ingredient in plasters for promoting suppuration. — Per., September.

S. aquaticus, Hill.—Water Ragwort. Ditches and wet situations.—Bi., July.

S. aquaticus, var. *pinnatifidus*, Gren. and Godr.—Wet ground, Kiloran.—August.

S. sarracenicus, L.—Broad-leaved Groundsel. Roadside near Tigh Samhraidh. It has been growing in the same place for a long time, and was probably planted about the beginning of last century.—Per., August.

Carlina, L.

C. vulgaris, L.—Common Carline. Fothannán Mín, I. Near the limestone rock, east side of Kiloran Bay, and a few plants on sandy hills, Balanahard.—Bi., July.

Arctium, L.

A. minus, Bernh. — Burdock. Mac-an-Dogha. Waste ground. The root was used in extracting-plasters.—Bi., July.

Cnicus, L.

The Melancholy Thistle (Cluas-an-Fhéidh), a species without prickles, is found in neighbouring islands.

C. lanceolatus, Willd.—Spear (plume) Thistle. Fòthannan (Glas). (An Cluaran Deilgneach.) Common in fields in rather dry situations.—Ann. or Bi., August.

C. palustris, Willd.—Marsh (plume) Thistle. Fòthannan (Leana). Common in wet situations. The leaves and root-stock are eaten in winter by sheep.—Bi., July.

C. arvensis, Hoffm.—Creeping (plume) Thistle. Fòthannan Achaidh. A troublesome weed of cultivated fields.—Per., July.

Centaurea, L.

Some species grown in gardens are herbaceous perennials with white, yellow, rose, violet, or purple coloured flowers; others, annuals, with blue and white flowers.

C. nigra, L. — Knapweed; Hardheads. Seamrag-nan-Each. Pastures.—Per., July.

Lapsana, L.

L. communis, L.—Nipplewort. Duilleag Mhaith; Duilleag Mhin, C. One specimen seen beside path in wood.—Ann., August.

Crepis, L.

C. capillaris, Wallr.—Smooth Hawk's-beard. Dry fields and sandy situations.—Ann. or Bi., July.

C. tectoria.—Alien. Turnip-field, Kiloran.

Hieracium, L.

A numerous and perplexing genus of perennial herbs. The latest (tenth) edition of the *London Catalogue of British Plants* enumerates about 300 species, varieties, and forms.

H. Pilosella, L.—Mouse-ear Hawkweed. Cluas Liath, C. Kiloran Bay.—June.

H. anglicum, Fr.—Hills above Port-Easdail.—August.

H. euprepes, c clivicolum, F. J. Hanb.—Ardskenish.—September. Confirmed by the late Rev. W. R. Linton.

H. dissimile, Lindeb.—Locality uncertain.

H. vulgatum, Fr. — Rocky ledge, northern exposure, Uragaig.—September.

H. vulgatum, d subravusculum, W. R. Linton.—Rocky ledge, Kiloran Bay.—September. Confirmed by the late Rev. W. R. Linton.

H. maculatum, Sm.—Top of old wall, Kiloran.—June.

H. strictum, Fr. — Rocky ledges, Balanahard hills. — September. Confirmed by the Rev. E. F. Linton.

H. sabaudum, L., *c rigens* (Jord.).—Ledges of rocks, Loch Fada side; northern exposure.—September. Confirmed by the Rev. W. R. Linton.

Hypochæris, L.

(?) *H. glabra,* L.—Smooth Cat's-ear. One plant, rocky hillock, Bealach-na-h-àirde.—October.

H. radicata, L.—Long-rooted Cat's-ear. Abundant in pastures and on rocky ledges throughout the island.—Per., July.

Leontodon, L.

L. autumnale, L.—Autumnal Hawkbit. Common on ledges of rocks and on an old wall in Kiloran.—Per., August. One of the specimens submitted to him was described by Mr Bennett as glabrous, single-bearded ; another as departing from the type towards the variety *linearifolius,* Brèb.

L. autumnale, b. pratense (Koch).—Locality uncertain. —September. Confirmed by Rev. E. F. Linton. Forms *simplex* and *glabrata* were recognised by Mr Bennett among specimens sent.

Taraxacum, Hall

T. officinale, Weber. — Common Dandelion. Beàrnan Brìde. Abundant. The roots and leaves were boiled and the decoction drunk.—Per. Flowering for a lengthened period. The roots have a bitter taste, and are tonic, aperient, and diuretic. Dried, roasted, and ground, they are sometimes mixed with coffee or even used as a substitute for it. The plant is cultivated and the leaves blanched for salad both in England and France.

T. erythrospermum, Andrz.—Not uncommon at Poll Gorm and at Cròisebrig, Balanahard.—May.

T. erythrospermum, b. lœvigatum (DC.).—East side of Traigh-nam-Bàrc.—May.

T. palustre, DC.—Balanahard hills.—July.

(?) *T. spectabile,* Dahlst.—Poll Gorm.—May. Material insufficient to be certain.

Sonchus, L.

S. oleraceus. L.—Common Sow-thistle. Bog-Fhonntan. Bainne Muice, I. A garden weed.—Ann., July. A very favourite food with hares and rabbits. W.

S. asper, Hill.—Prickly Sow-thistle. Searbhán Muc, I. Commoner than the preceding species. A very prickly form is met with on the sandy shores.—Ann., July.

S. arvensis, L.—Corn Sow-thistle. Bliochd Fochainn, C. A conspicuous cornfield weed.—Per., September. The flowers regularly follow the course of the sun. W.

CAMPANULACEÆ (the Campanula family)

Principally herbs, including many beautiful garden flowering plants.

Lobelia, L.

The pretty dwarf Lobelias so much used for bedding are varieties and hybrids raised from blue and white South African species—*L. erinus*, *L. bicolor*, etc. *L. cardinalis* from Virginia, usually treated as half-hardy, has locally proved hardy.

L. Dortmanna, L.—Water Lobelia. Plùr-an-Lochain, C. Shallow waters, edge of Loch Fada—Per., June.

Jasione, L.

J. montana, L. — Sheep's-bit. Dubhan-nan-Caora, C. Recorded by Messrs Grieve and Somerville.

Campanula, L.

A numerous genus with many garden representatives— *C. medium* (Canterbury Bell), *C. pyramidalis*, *C. persicifolia*, etc.—that greatly contribute to the beauty of the greenhouse and the herbaceous border. The Garden Rampion (Meacan Raibe Fiadhain (?), I.) is cultivated for its fleshy root.

C. rotundifolia, L.—Common Harebell ; Scottish Bluebell. Broga-Cuthaig. Am Pluran Cluigeannach, C. Broga-Cuthaig is also locally applied to the Pansy and the Dog Violet. Common on dry rocky ledges. White forms have been seen.—Per., August.

VACCINIACEÆ (the Cranberry family)

The Cowberry (Dearc-Mhonaidh) and Cranberry (Muileag ; Geàrr-Dhearc), common in the Highlands, bear edible fruit. The Bogberry (Dearc Roide, C. ; Móineóg, I.) is said, when eaten, to cause headache.

Vaccinium, L.

V. Myrtillus, L.—Blaeberry ; Whortleberry. Dearca Coille. Abundant, Coille - mhor. Berries edible.—May. The plant (with alum) yields a blue dye. The first tender leaves cannot be distinguished from real tea when properly gathered and dried. W. Dearcan Fithich, C.

ERICACEÆ (the Heath family)

Shrubs of low growth, often growing on moors and hills in peaty soil. The foliage of some species—Rhododendrons, Azaleas, etc.—is poisonous. The briar-root of commerce, for making pipes, is the wood of the Tree Heath, a native of the south of Europe. This order includes some pretty greenhouse and garden shrubs — Indian Rhododendrons, American Azaleas, etc. The Strawberry Tree (Caithne, C.) is confined to Ireland.

Arctostaphylos, Adans.

A. Uva-ursi, Spreng.—Bearberry. Braoileag. Among the heather on dry, rocky hills.—May.

Calluna, Salisb.

C. vulgaris, Hull.—Common Ling or Heather. Fraoch. By far the commonest species. Used for making door-mats, brooms, ropes for fixing on thatch, etc. A green dye (with alum) is obtained from it. Heather ale is said to have been formerly made from the green tops. Miona (meanbh) Fhraoch = the young growth after the old heather is burned. Cattle prefer it to the older growth, and it forms the principal food of grouse. White forms (Fraoch Geal) are not uncommon.—August. This is the most widely distributed of all the heaths. The badge of the Macdonalds. Fraoch Badanach (?). Fraoch Gorm, C.

Erica, L.

A numerous genus of more than 400 species (mostly from South-West Africa), besides innumerable cultivated hybrids and varieties.

E. Tetralix, L.—Cross-leaved Heath. Fraoch Gucanach. Heaths and wet moors. This, owing to its fine wiry nature, is the kind most preferred for brooms, scouring-brushes, etc. —July. Fraoch-an-Ruinnse, C.

E. cinerea, L.—Scottish Heather ; Bell Heather. Fraoch Meangan. White forms of this species and E. Tetralix are seen.—August. Badge of the Robertsons. Fraoch Seangan. Fraoch-a'-Bhadain, C.

Pyrola, L.

P. media, Sw.—Recorded by Mr Somerville.

P. minor, L. — Common Wintergreen. Near Slochd-an-Fhomhair. — Per., June. A small colony on an exposed headland, Uragaig, did not flower in 1908 ; the species was not determined. P. minor was recorded by Mr. Ewing from Jura in 1888.

PLUMBAGINACEÆ (the Plumbago family)

Principally herbs, with bitter or acrid properties.

Statice, Linn.

S. maritima, L.—Thrift ; Sea Pink. Neòinean Cladaich. Abundant on the sea rocks and on the shore turf.—Per., May.

PRIMULACEÆ (the Primrose family)

Herbs, excelling in the beauty of their flowers. The Auricula (Lus-na-Ban-Righ, C.), Sow-bread (Culurin, C.),

Shieldworts, etc., are represented in gardens by many pretty varieties.

Primula, L.

A genus of plants including lovely alpine species. The Cowslip (Mùisean) and the Oxlip (Bugha Geal, I.) are British natives. Wine is made from the flowers of the Cowslip. *P. sinensis* from China and *P. japonica* from Japan are old greenhouse favourites.

P. vulgaris, Huds.—Primrose. Sobhrachan. Samharcan, C. Edges of woods and shady slopes and banks. Used as an ingredient in healing ointments.—Per., May.

"Sobhrachan, Samhrachan, Biadh-ùr-Eunachan, is maith am biadh
  pàisd, e ;
  Grainnseagan 's Dearca Coille, biadh na cloinne san t-samhradh."
                                   (Children's rhyme ; local.)

An agreeable wine is prepared from Primroses, not very unlike that made from Cowslips, but considered still more delicate in flavour.

Lysimachia, L.

L. punctata, Linn.—Yellow Loosestrife. Introduced, and grown in gardens.
L. nemorum, L.—Yellow Pimpernel. (Seamrag Mhuire.) Damp situations, Kiloran woods.—Per., July.

Glaux, L.

G. maritima, L. — Sea Milkwort ; Black Saltwort. In plenty on the shore turf, Traigh-nam-Bàrc, and wedged in between the joints of the phyllites, Port - an - Obain, Balanahard. Common seashore plant.—Per., June.

Anagallis, L.

A. arvensis, L.—Scarlet Pimpernel ; Poor Man's Weather-glass. (Falcair-Fiadhain.) Cornfields, etc.—Ann., July. On

the approach of rain the petals close. Farcuire Fuar, I.
Formerly used medicinally as a purgative. C. This
species, like the common Chickweed, has accompanied man
in his migrations over a great part of the globe.

A. tenella, Murr.—Bog Pimpernel. Common on mossy
banks and in wet situations.—Per., July.

Centunculus, L.

C. minimus, L.—Small Chaffweed ; Bastard Pimpernel.
Traigh Staosnaig and Balanahard. — August. This little
annual, which has not yet, probably on account of its
smallness, been recorded from the neighbouring islands,
has a wide distribution over Europe, Russian Asia, North
America, and Australia.

Samolus, L.

S. Valerandi, L.—Brookweed. Edges of stony shallow
streams, particularly at the shore.—Per., July.

OLEACEÆ (the Olive family)

The order is represented in shrubberies by the Lilac
(Craobh Liath-ghorm, C.), Jasmine, etc. The Privet (Ras
Chrann Sìor-uaine ; Priobhadh, C.) is much used for hedges,
and thrives well in towns. The Olive (Crann Oladh), a
native of Syria and Greece, yields the valuable Olive oil.
The branch of the Olive signifies peace and plenty.

Fraxinus, L.

F. excelsior, L.—Ash. Uinnseann. One of the commonest
planted trees in Kiloran plantations, and growing naturally
from seed. Some trees are also to be seen in Glaic-an-
Uinnsinn which are possibly indigenous. Wood used
locally for tool-handles, swingle-trees, etc.—May. Tough
and elastic, it was formerly selected for spear-handles, as

10

now it is the wood used for the lance-shafts of the British cavalry. The wood of the American Ash (*F. americana*, L.), though largely imported into this country for agricultural implements, tool-handles, etc., is inferior to the British Ash. The leaves act like Senna.

APOCYNACEÆ (the Periwinkle family)

A large tropical order; some species yielding milky, elastic, and sometimes very poisonous juices, while others furnish edible fruits, oil, medicine, etc. The Silk Rubber Tree of Lagos is one of the most important sources of West African rubber. The order furnishes some beautiful stove plants— Allamandas, Dipladenias, etc. The South European Oleander is an old greenhouse favourite.

Vinca, L.

V. minor, L.—Lesser Periwinkle.   Gille-Fionndruinn. Introduced.—May.   Badge of the M'Lachlans.

GENTIANACEÆ (the Gentian family)

Herbs, occurring principally in temperate and mountainous regions, where some species mark the highest limits of vegetation. They are characterised by powerfully bitter properties, and are universally used as febrifugal and stomachic medicines. Some species (Gentians) are among the prettiest of alpine plants.

Centaurium, Hill

C. umbellatum, Gilib. — Centaury.   Deagha Dearg, I. Sandy uncultivated hillocks, Druim-buidhe.—Bi., July.

C. umbellatum, *b capitatum*.   Close to the shore, Port-a-Bhuailtein.—September.

Gentiana, L.

G. Amarella, L.—Autumn Gentian. Machrins golf-links, and sandy pasture, Balanahard Bay.—Ann., August.

G. campestris, L.—Field Gentian. Lus-a-Chrùbain. Frequent in moist pastures.—Ann., August. This plant acts as an excellent tonic. It is believed to be a good remedy for the disease called "crùban" in cattle. C.

G. baltica, Murb.—Dry, sandy, uncultivated hillocks, Ardskenish Glen.—August.

Menyanthes, L.

M. trifoliata, L.—Buckbean; Bog Bean. Luibh-nan-tri-Beann. Common at the edges of the lochs. An infusion of the stem and leaves is a popular remedy for a weak stomach, the stem being also chewed for the same purpose.—Per., June.

POLEMONIACEÆ (the Polemonium family)

Principally herbs, including the beautiful perennial Phloxes and annual Gilias.

Polemonium, L.

P. cœruleum, L.—Jacob's Ladder; Greek Valerian. Introduced, and grown in gardens.

BORAGINACEÆ (the Borage family)

Herbs, usually with roughly hairy stems and leaves, and the flowers in one-sided spikes. Their properties are mucilaginous and cooling, and the roots of some kinds (Alkanet, etc.) yield a dye. The mucilage from the root of the Comfrey (Meacan Dubh; Lus-nan-Cnamh-briste, C.) was formerly considered a good remedy for uniting broken bones. The Peruvian Heliotrope has long been grown for its sweet perfume. Species of North American Nemophilas are showy dwarf annuals. *N. insignis* has large, distinct, sky-blue flowers.

Borago, L.

B. officinalis, L.—Borage. (Borraidh.) Introduced.—Ann. or Bi., July. A native of the east Mediterranean region, it has, by long cultivation, become naturalised in various parts of England. The flowers are used for garnishing, and the young leaves employed in salads and also pickled. A good honey-producing plant, it is sometimes sown for bees.

Anchusa, L.

A. officinalis, L.—Common Alkanet. Recorded by Messrs Grieve and Miller.

Lycopsis, L.

L. arvensis, L.—Small Bugloss. Lus-Teang'-an-Daimh, C. A weed of sandy cultivated fields.—Ann., July.

Myosotis, L.

Early flowering and hardy, some kinds are commonly utilised in " spring bedding " arrangements.

M. cœspitosa, Schultz.—Forget-me-not ; Scorpion-grass. Còbharach. Cotharach, C. Locally used as an emblem of good luck.—Per., July.

M. palustris, Hill.—Recorded by Mr Grieve.

M. repens, G. and D. Don.—" This is the chief Forget-me-not of the island, flowering a little earlier than *cœspitosa* " (Somerville).—Per., June.

M. sylvatica, Hoffm.—Neighbourhood of garden, Kiloran. Introduced.—May.

M. arvensis, Hill. — Cultivated ground, Geadhail-na-Cèardach.—Ann., June.

M. collina, Hoffm.—Recorded by Mr Grieve.

M. versicolor, Sm.—Changing Forget-me-not. Un-cultivated hillocks ; common.—Ann., June.

M. versicolor, var. *laxa*, Bosch.—Slender form, cultivated field, Kiloran.

CONVOLVULACEÆ (the Convolvulus family)

Herbs, twining or prostrate, often with handsome plaited flowers. The most important species of the family is *Ipomœa Batatas* (Sweet Potato). Jalep, the well-known purgative, is prepared from the root of a Mexican plant. Annual kinds of Convolvulus are showy climbing objects. The Seaside Convolvulus occurs in the Outer Hebrides in the island of Eriskay, where it is supposed to have been planted by Prince Charlie—hence known there as Flùr-a-Phrionnsa (the Prince's flower).

Calystegia, Br.

C. sepium, Br.—Larger Convolvulus ; Hooded Bindweed. Duil Mhial, C. Roadside, Glasaird —Per., August.

Convolvulus, L.

C. arvensis, L.—Small Bindweed. Iadh-lus, C. Lower Kilchattan.—July.

SOLANACEÆ (the Nightshade family)

A large order of herbs and shrubs, chiefly tropical. Many are characterised by dangerous and narcotic properties ; others, as the Tomato, Egg-plant, Potato (Buntata), etc., furnish wholesome fruit or tubers. Tobacco (Tombaca) was brought to this country shortly after the middle of the sixteenth century. Cayenne Pepper (Peabar Dearg) is the powdered seed of species of Capsicum. The root of the Mandrake (Mandrag) was credited by the ancients with many virtues. British species—the Deadly Nightshade

(Lus-na-Díbh-Mór, I.), Henbane (Caothach-nan-Cearc), Thorn-apple—have very poisonous properties. The "Tea Plant," a straggling shrub, is recommended for situations exposed to the sea-breezes.

Solanum, L.

A numerous genus, particularly abundant in South America. *S. tuberosum* (the Potato) is a native of Chili and Peru, where it is found growing on sterile mountains and in damp forests near the sea. According to some it was introduced to this country by Sir Walter Raleigh (from Virginia, in 1586); in the opinion of others, by Sir Francis Drake. The numerous excellent varieties now in cultivation have sprung from a few comparatively worthless wild species. At the Franco-British Exhibition in London (1908) no less than 300 selected kinds (named) were exhibited by Messrs Sutton & Sons. The same firm showed a number of wild types at the R.H.S. Temple Show in May 1907.

S. Dulcamara, L.—Bittersweet. Fuath-gorm, C. Burnside, Kiloran, and gullies, Kiloran Bay.—Per., July. The berries are bitter and poisonous. The root and stem have a bitter taste followed by a degree of sweetness, hence the common English name. A decoction of the plant is said to be good for internal injuries.

SCROPHULARIACEÆ (the Scrophularia family)

One of the most largely represented of British orders, remarkable for many beautiful flowering species. They are generally acrid or bitter, and sometimes, as in the Foxglove, poisonous. Representatives of exotic (Calceolaria, Pentstemon, Mimulus, etc.) and native genera (Speedwell, Toadflax, Mullein, Snapdragon, etc.) are old favourites. Some kinds—Lousewort, Yellow Rattle, Eyebright, and Cow-wheat are semi-parasitical.

Verbascum, L.

V. var.—Mullein. Cow's Lungwort. Coinneal Mhuire, C. Introduced, and growing naturally from seed, Kiloran.

Antirrhinum, L.

A. var.—Snapdragon. Sriumh-na-Laogh, C. Top of garden wall.—Per., July.

Scrophularia, L.

S. nodosa, L.—Figwort. (Lus-nan-Cnapan ; Farach Dubh.) Gully below Tigh Iain Daraich.—Per., August. The name is derived from scrofula, for which species of the genus were considered an excellent remedy. *S. nodosa* was formerly employed in medicine as an emetic and purgative.

Mimulus, L.

M. luteus, Willd.—Yellow Mimulus. Burnside, Kiloran. —Per., August. Originally a native of North-West America and Chili, it has now become naturalised in many parts of the country.

Digitalis, L.

D. purpurea, L.—Foxglove. Meuran-nan-Daoine-Marbh. Abundant in dry situations at the roadside, in the woods, and on the hills. Sithean-as-nach-cinn is the name locally applied to the first year's growth of this species, one of the herbs frequently used in poultices. Damh-donn is believed to apply to the same plant. White forms only seen occasion-ally.—Bi. or Per., July. It contains a powerful poison, used in medicine as a diuretic and sedative.

Veronica, L.

Beautiful hybrids with white, purple, blue, red, or crimson flowers have been obtained from New Zealand shrubby species —*V. speciosa, V. salicifolia* (both locally hardy), and others.

V. hederæfolia, L.—Ivy-leaved Speedwell. Garden weed, Kiloran.—Ann., May.

V. polita, Fr.—Old wall, Kiloran.—Ann., May.

V. agrestis, L.—Procumbent Speedwell. Common weed of cultivated fields on the raised-beach deposits.—Ann., May.

V. Tournefortii, C. Gmel.—Garden weed, Benoran.—Ann., May.

V. peregrina, L.—A few plants on gravel-walk, Kiloran garden.—Ann., June. "A native of America; now a weed in Ireland, Spain, Belgium, Holland, Germany, and Italy. In Great Britain it was first observed near Belfast in Ireland" (A. B.).

V. arvensis, L.—Wall Veronica. Abundant on old walls, in pastures, etc.—Ann., July.

V. arvensis, L., *b nana*, Poir.—Hollow in the blown sands, Balanahard Bay.—May.

V. serpyllifolia, L.—Smooth-leaved Speedwell. Hills above mill; common.—Per., May.

V. officinalis, L.—Common Speedwell. (Lus crè.) Dry slopes.—Per. The leaves have a slight degree of astringency and bitterness.

V. Chamædrys, L.—Germander Speedwell. Nuallach, I. Abundant all over the island.—Per., May.

V. scutellata, L.—Marsh Speedwell. Marshy ground, Pairc Bhaile Mhaide; rare.—Per., June.

V. Beccabunga, L.—Brooklime. Lochal, C. Biolair Mhuire, I. Muddy places in various localities.—Per., September.

Euphrasia, L.

Herbs, the British species of which are annual, and semi-parasitic on the roots of grasses. Their tendency to hybridise increases the difficulties of correct determination. The following were kindly named by the Rev. E. S. Marshall, M.A., F.L.S., from dried specimens collected in July and August. *E. borealis*, Towns., abundant on wet ground in some of the islands, is not included in the local list.

E. Rostkoviana, Hayne.—Mr Ewing believed some specimens submitted to answer the description of this species. Mr M'Vicar found it a common plant on the West Coast.

E. brevipila, Burnat and Gremli.—Eyebright. Briollan. (Lus-nan-Leac.) Balaromin-dubh.—August. One of the commonest kinds in pastures. An infusion of this and other species was believed to be beneficial as an application to sore eyes.

E. gracilis, Fr.—A slender species, found in wet situations on hilly ground.

E. curta, Wettst., *b. glabrescens*, Wettst.—Frequent on sandy, hilly ground near the shore.

Bartsia, L.

B. Odontites, Huds.—Red Bartsia. Moist situations in fields and pastures.—Ann., July. It is half parasitical on the roots of other plants.

B. Odontites, var. *verna*.—Noted by Mr Somerville.

B. Odontites, *d. litoralis*, Reichb.—Growing down close to the sea rocks, Port Mor. " This var. was found by Mr Symers Macvicar at Mingary Bay, Ardnamurchan, Argyll shire, in July 1896 and sent to me. Since, it has only occurred near Wick in Caithness in 1906. It occurs in Denmark, Sweden, Norway, Finland, etc." (A. B.).

Pedicularis, L.

P. palustris, L.—Marsh Lousewort ; Red Rattle. Lus Riabhach ; Modhalan Dearg, C. Marshes, sides of ditches, etc. A taller and later flowering plant, it is hardly so plentiful as the following species.—Bi., July.

P. sylvatica, L.—Lousewort. Lus-na-Meala ; Bainne-bò-Gamhnach ; Bainne Crodh Laoigh. Abundant in peaty pastures.—Bi. or Per., May. In olden times it was believed that the plant caused animals which grazed on it to become subject to parasites (hence the common English name), the poor condition of the animals being really due to the inferior pasturage in which the plant grows. The Gaelic names, on the other hand, were derived from the honey secreted in the flowers, which children were in the habit of sucking.

Rhinanthus, L.

R. Crista-galli, L.—Yellow Rattle. Gleadhran. Abundant in poor meadows.—Ann., June. This plant has short fibrous roots which become attached to the living roots of grasses and other plants by means of suckers. These abstract nourishment from the host plants ; and where it is abundant, as at Crosan, the hay crop is invariably light. Modhalan Buidhe, C.

Melampyrum, L.

M. pratense, L.—Cowwheat. Not uncommon in dry situations on the hilly ground.—Ann., July.

Orobanchaceæ (the Broomrape family)

A small order of parasitical herbs. The Toothwort is a parasite often growing in Britain on the roots of the Hazel.

Orobanche, L.

O. rubra, Sm.—Red Broomrape. Muchóg, I. Neighbourhood of Kiloran Bay, growing on the roots of the Wild Thyme. A brittle plant, it is frequently broken down by sheep.—Per., June.

Lentibulariaceæ (the Pinguicula family)

Marsh or aquatic plants with spurred flowers.

Utricularia, L.

U. major, Schmidel.—Common Bladderwort. In deep water, west Loch Fada.—Per., July.

U. minor, L.—Common in peat-holes on the moors.—July.
U. intermedia, Hayne.—Peat-bogs, Kilchattan hills.

Pinguicula, L.

P. vulgaris, L.—Butterwort. Modalan. (Badan Meas-gan.) Frequent on wet banks. This plant, together with the Whin and Juniper, was believed to act as a charm against witchcraft. Cows that ate it were safe from elfish arrows and supernatural ailments that were supposed to make much havoc in olden times. It was believed that a healthy, nice-looking baby was sometimes coveted and, when the opportunity occurred, even carried off by the fairies and a languishing, old-fashioned creature left in its place. Some women, as the story goes, who were watching a new-born infant in a house in Machrins to make sure that the child would not be changed, heard two fairies coming to the window, and the following conversation take place. " We will take it," said one. " We will not, we cannot," said the other ; " its mother partook of the butter of the cow that ate the Butterwort."—Per., June. It is said to possess the property of coagulating milk.

P. lusitanica. L.—Pale Butterwort. Not uncommon in peat-bogs.—Per., August.

LABIATÆ (the Labiate family)

A large order, comprising upwards of 3000 species, wholly devoid of hurtful properties. Aromatic oil is secreted in the glands of the leaves of many, which render them valuable as stimulants, flavouring herbs, ingredients of perfumes, etc. Marjoram (Oragan, C.), Savory (Garbhag Gàraidh), Hyssop (Isop), Sage (Saitse), etc., are cultivated as pot-herbs. In addition to being used for stuffing, Sage was formerly in demand as tea. Lavender (Lus-na-Tùise, C.), Rosemary (Corr-Lus), etc., are largely used in the preparation of perfumes. Lavender is cultivated in Surrey and Lincolnshire for the flowers from which the oil is distilled. A decoction of the leaves of Rosemary is said to relieve headaches, and also to promote the growth of hair and cure baldness. The leaves and tops of Horehound (Grafan Ban, C.), in addition to possessing tonic and laxative properties, have long been a popular remedy for asthma and coughs. The beverage Horehound beer is made from it. *Salvia splendens* (brilliant scarlet), *S. patens* (lovely blue), and many other species decorate gardens.

Mentha, L.

Various species—Pennyroyal (Borragach, I.), Peppermint, Spearmint, etc.—have long been cultivated as carminative aromatics. For culinary purposes Spearmint is preferred, as in sauces, salads, etc.; but for medicine Peppermint and Pennyroyal are more efficacious. A conserve of the leaves is very grateful, and the distilled waters, both simple and spirituous, are very agreeable. The virtues of Mint are those of warm stomachic and carminative. For winter use the herb should be cut in a very dry season, and just when they are in flower; if cut in the wet they will turn black and be of little worth. W.

M. spicata, L.—Spearmint. Cartal Gàraidh. (Mionnt Gàraidh.) Site of old garden, Pairc-dhubh. Cultivated in gardens.—Per., August.

M. piperita, L.—Peppermint. (Mionntuinn.) Burnside, Kiloran Bay. Formerly grown in Kiloran garden for the distillation of peppermint cordial for medicinal use.—Per., August.

M. aquatica, L., *a hirsuta* (Huds.).—Water Mint. Cartal Uisge. This kind (irrespective of variety), was collected in summer and used for flavouring both in the green state and dried. A few sprigs were tied with a piece of thread and immersed in the vessel with the food that was cooking until it was sufficiently flavoured. (*M. hirsuta*, Rev. E. F. Linton.)—Per., August.

M. aquatica, L., × *arvensis*.—Moist ground west of pond, Kiloran. (*M. sativa*, Rev. E. F. Linton.)

M. aquatica, L., × *arvensis*, *b paludosa* (Sole).—Ditch, Ceann-da-Lèana; September. (*M. paludosa*, Rev. E. F. Linton.)

(?) *M. gentilis*, L. — Vicinity of garden, Kiloran.— September.

M. arvensis, L.—Corn Mint. (Mionnt-an-Arbhair.) Cornfield, Uragaig Bheag.—Per., August.

Lycopus, L.

L. europœus, L.—Gipsywort. Feorán Curraigh, I. In moist gullies on the eastern shore, in the neighbourhood of Loch Fada, and other places.—Per., July. It dyes black. The juice gives a permanent colour to linen, wool, and silk, which will not wash out. W.

Thymus, L.

The common garden Thyme (Tím, I.), used in soups and for stuffings, etc., is a native of the south of Europe.

T. serpyllum, L.—Wild Thyme. Luibh-na-Machrach. (Lus-Mhic-Righ-Bhreatuinn.) Dry and sandy situations, especially near the shore. It was much used for making tea. —Per., August. This plant had the reputation of giving courage and strength through its smell. Highlanders take an infusion of it to prevent disagreeable dreams. C. The dried leaves, used instead of tea, are exceedingly grateful and a good stomachic ; the tops dye purple. W.

Melissa, I.

M. officinalis, L.—Common Balm. Lus-na-Malla, I. Introduced and formerly used for making tea.—Per., July.

Scutellaria, L.

S. galericulata, L.—Common Skullcap. Stony shores, Slochd-an-Fhomhair, and eastern side of the island.—Per., September.

S. minor, Huds.—Lesser Skullcap. Common in moist situations in the hilly pastures.—September.

Prunella, L.

P. vulgaris, L. — Self-heal. Ceann-a-Sgadain-Dheirg. Ceanabhan Beag, C. Abundant; white forms not uncommon. A popular remedy for chest ailments, it was collected in summer, tied in bundles, and hung up to the kitchen roof to dry for winter use. The plants were boiled in milk and strained before using; butter was added.—Per., August.

Stachys, L.

S. palustris, L.—Marsh Woundwort. Brisgean-nan-Caorach. A troublesome weed found in badly drained places in cultivated fields. Sheep are fond of the fleshy rhizomes.— Per., September. The roots have also been used for the table. The plant was formerly held in high repute for wound-healing and blood-stopping qualities.

S. sylvatica, L.—Hedge Woundwort. (Lus-nan-Sgor.) A coarse, hairy perennial with a fetid scent; not uncommon on banks at the roadside, Kiloran.—August.

S. arvensis, L.—Corn Woundwort. A common weed of cultivated fields.—Ann., August.

Galeopsis, L.

G. speciosa, Mill.—An Gath Buidhe, C. Cultivated fields.—Ann., September.

G. Tetrahit, L.—Common Hemp Nettle. Feanndag Nimhneach. An Gath Dubh, C. A common cornfield weed —Ann., September.

Lamium, L.

L. amplexicaule, L.—Henbit. Neanntóg Chaoch, I. Recorded by Mr Somerville.

L. molucellifolium, Fr.—Common garden weed.—Ann., June.

L. purpureum, L.—Red Dead-nettle. Neanntag Aog. A weed of gardens and fields.—Ann., June.

Teucrium, L.

T. Scorodonia, L.—Wood Sage. Saitse Fiadhaich. Abundant in dry, rocky situations on the east side of the island.— Per., August.

Ajuga, L.

A. reptans, L.—Creeping Bugle. Meacan Dubh Fiadhain, C. Abundant, and thinly carpeting the ground with its runners, under the trees in Kiloran woods.—Per., May. It was formerly used as a vulnerary, and possesses a considerable degree of astringency. In olden times it was used as a specific in gout, jaundice, and other complaints.

A. pyramidalis, L. — Erect Bugle. Rocky crevices, Balanahard. The plants were much eaten by sheep or rabbits.—Bi. or Per., May.

PLANTAGINACEÆ (the Plantain family)

A small order, occurring in greatest abundance in the temperate regions of the Old World.

Plantago, L.

P. major, L.—Greater Plantain; Way-bread. Cuach Phàruig. One of the principal ingredients used locally in extracting-plasters. The leaf was sometimes warmed, beaten between the palms, and the ribs pulled out to make them smooth for applying to boils after they commenced to run.

—Per., September. The fruiting spikes are gathered in the green state and used for feeding caged birds.

P. lanceolata, L.—Ribwort Plantain; Rib Grass. Slanlus. Abundant in pastures, and one of the most commonly used herbs for medicinal purposes. It was pounded into pulp and laid over wounds and used as an ingredient in the healing ointments.—Bi. or Per., July. It was formerly cultivated on the mainland as a forage plant.

P. maritima, L.—Seaside Plantain. Feur Saille. Common at the seaside. Cattle are fond of it, and it is believed to improve the yield of cream and butter. It was gathered for pet rabbits.—Per., July.

P. maritima, var. *glabrata.*—Uragaig shore. September.

P. coronopus, L.—Buckshorn Plantain. Star of the Earth. Abundant in dry situations near the shore.—Bi., July. It was formerly cultivated in this country for the leaves, which were used in salads; it is still grown in France.

Littorela, Bergius.

L. uniflora, Aschers.—Shore-weed. Abundant along the shallow, stony margins of the lochs.—Per., July.

ILLECEBRACEÆ (the Illebrecum family).

Weedy herbs or shrubs abounding in the more sterile tracts of temperate regions.

Scleranthus, L.

S. annuus, L.—Knawel. Cobhair Mhuire, I. A small annual of fields and waste places, recorded by Mr Somerville.

AMARANTHACEÆ (the Amaranthus family)

A large tropical order, several foreign species of which are becoming naturalised in this country. Tender varieties— Love-lies-Bleeding (Lus-a-Ghraidh, C.), Prince's Feather, Cockscomb—are grown in gardens.

Amaranthus, L.

A. sp.—Vacant ground, Kiloran ; introduced with feeding-stuffs.—Ann., August.

CHENOPODIACEÆ (the Goosefoot family)

A large order growing in waste places and within the influence of a saline atmosphere. Some possess medicinal properties, and others—Spinach (Spionáiste ; Lus Míne, I.), Beet, etc.—are cultivated as kitchen garden esculents. Maritime species were formerly valued for the quantity of soda contained in their ashes.

Chenopodium, L.

A rather large genus of herbs. The farinaceous seeds of *C. Quinoa* are an important article of food to the inhabitants of Peru, and it is sometimes cultivated in gardens and the leaves used like Spinach. Good King Henry, All-good (Praiseach Bràthair, C.), was formerly much used as a pot-herb.

C. album, L.—White Goosefoot. Càl Slapach. Waysides. The leaves were boiled, pounded, buttered, and eaten like Spinach.—Ann., August.

Beta, L.

B. maritima, L.—Common Beet. (Biotais.) A few plants on the rocky shore near Carraig Chatan.—Per., June. The sugar and garden varieties of Beet and the Mangold Wurzel are improved forms of the wild species.

Atriplex, L.

A large genus, generally common in maritime regions. *A. hortensis* (Orache), a native of Tartary, is cultivated for its leaves.

A. patula, L.—Common Orache. Praiseach Mhin, C.

11

Stony shore, Scalasaig harbour.—Ann., August. It is sometimes gathered as a pot-herb and eaten in lieu of Spinach
and other greens. W.

A. patula, b. erecta, Huds.—A more erect form than the
type abundant at Port Mor.

A. patula, c. angustifolia (Sm.). — Recorded by Messrs
Grieve and Miller.

A. Babingtonii, Woods.—Seashores.—Ann., August.

A. Babingtonii, b. virescens, Lange.—Shore, Balaromin-
dubh.

A. laciniata, L.—Frosted Orache. Kiloran Bay sands;
a few plants.—Ann., August.

A. Smithii, Syme.—Port Mor shore.—September.

Salicornia, L.

S. europœa, L.—Glasswort. Praiseach-na-Mara, C. Salt-
marsh, Strand and Port-an-Obain, Scalasaig.—Ann., September.

Suœda, Forsk.

S. maritima, Dum., *b. procumbens*, Syme. — Sea-Blite.
Plentiful north of the harbour.—Ann., August.

Salsola, L.

S. Kali, L.—Prickly Saltwort. Sandy shores.—Ann.,
August.

POLYGONACEÆ (the Buckwheat family)

A large order, mostly herbaceous plants, readily known
by a membraneous sheath round the stem, at the base of the
leaf-stalk. The foliage of some have an acid juice; others
are strongly astringent. The roots are often purgative.
Many, such as the Knot-grass and Dock, are common and
troublesome weeds. The best-known plants of the family
are the garden Rhubarb (Lus-na-Purgaid) and Buckwheat,
the latter largely cultivated on the Continent and in North

America for its farinaceous seeds, from which an excellent bread is made. Medicinal Rhubarb is obtained from the dried roots of various species of Rheum, natives of China and Tibet.

Polygonum, L.

P. Convolvulus, L.—Climbing Buckwheat. Casraiginn. A weed of cultivated fields.—Ann., July.

P. Convolvulus, L., *b subalatum*, V. Hall.—Garden weed, Kiloran.—October.

P. aviculare, L.—Bird's Knotgrass. Glùineach Bheag, C. Shingly shores, edges of fields, etc. Grazing animals are fond of it.—Ann., July.

P. Raii, Bab.—One plant ; locality uncertain.

P. Hydropiper, L. — Water-pepper. Glùineach Theth ; Lus-an-Fhògair, C. Ditches and edges of pools.—Ann., August. The whole plant has an acrid, burning taste ; it dyes wool yellow. W.

P. Persicaria, L.—Spotted Knotweed. Glùineach Dhearg. A common weed of cultivated fields.—Ann., July. Lus Chroinn-ceusaidh (the legend being that this plant grew at the foot of the Cross, and drops of blood fell on the leaves, and so they are spotted to this day). C.

P. amphibium, L.—Amphibious Buckwheat. Glùineach Uisge. Abundant in wet situations, and also frequently seen in comparatively dry places.—Per., August.

Rumex, L.

Perennials, with a thick root-stock. Several kinds, as the French and the Mountain Sorrel, are grown for their leaves, which are used in soups, salads, and sauces. The roots of an American species are used for tanning. *R. Patientia* (Patience) was formerly much grown for its leaves.

R. conglomeratus, Murr. — Clustered Dock. Moist gullies, Kiloran Bay and Ardskenish Glen.—August.

R. obtusifolius, L.—Broad Dock. Vacant ground, Kiloran.—August. Fallow deer eat this species with avidity, eating it close to the root, so that it is very rare to see a Dock growing in a deer park. W.

R. obtusifolius, sub. sp. *R. Friesii*, Gren. and Godr.—Kiloran.—September.

R. crispus, L.—Curled Dock. Copag. Common on the shore, growing down to the tide-mark.—August.

R. crispus, L., var. *littoreus*, Hardy.—Waste places.—September.

R. Acetosa, L.—Sorrel. Samh; Sealbhag. Abundant in moist situations. Used locally for taking rust out of linen, and employed in the process of dyeing with indigo.—July. The leaves, which are powerfully acid, are eaten in sauces and salads. W. Slochd-na-Sealbhag, Balanahard.

R. Acetosella, L.—Sheep's Sorrel. Ruanaidh, C. Dry hillocks.—August.

ELÆAGNACEÆ (the Oleaster family)

A small order of trees and shrubs, represented in Britain by one species. Buffalo Berries, used for preserves, are produced by a spiny North American shrub.

Hippophœ, L.

H. Rhamnoides, L.—Sea Buckthorn. Planted for screening young plantations, and now spreading (by suckers).

The Common Mistletoe (Druidhlus, I.) is the only British representative of the next order, Loranthaceæ, a family of half-succulent evergreens which are parasitical on trees. The Mistletoe grows on the Apple, Thorn, Oak, Lime, etc., in the south of England. It was regarded with great veneration by the Druids, who believed it would cure all manner of diseases. When found growing on the Oak, it was, with great ceremony, cut by a Druid clothed in a white robe, with a golden sickle, and a sacrifice of two white bulls offered on the spot.

EUPHORBIACEÆ (the Spurge family)

An important tropical order, most of the species containing lactiferous vessels with a milky fluid, often dangerously poisonous (Manchineel, etc.), sometimes valuable as rubber. The seeds of exotic species contain oil—Castor oil, Croton oil. Other species are valued for their timber, edible fruits, and nuts. A large Brazilian tree yields the Para rubber. Tapioca is obtained from the roots of the Bitter Cassava, a plant so highly poisonous that animals which drink of the water where the roots have been washed and scraped often die. The poison (prussic acid) is dispelled by heat. In China, candles are made from solid oil contained in the seeds of the Tallow tree. The seeds of the Candle-nut tree are strung on pieces of bamboo by natives of the South Sea Islands and burned like candles. Dwarf forms of the Common Box (Bocsa) (which differs from most plants of the order in the absence of milky juice) are used for edging garden walks. Brilliant flowered and beautifully variegated foliaged species (Poinsettias, Crotons) are grown in hot-houses.

Euphorbia, L.

E. Helioscopia, L.—Sun Spurge. Cranntachan-an-Deamh-ain. Foinne-lus, C. Cultivated fields. The milky juice was applied to warts.—Ann., August.

E. Peplus, L.—Petty Spurge. (Lus Leigheis.) Garden weed, Kiloran.—Ann., September.

Mercurialis, L.

M. perennis, L.—Perennial Mercury. (Lus-Ghlinn-Bhràca-dail.) Recorded by Messrs Grieve and Miller. It was formerly much used for the cure of wounds. C.

URTICACEÆ (the Nettle family)

A large order, of warm climates, with leaves often rough or stinging, and small unisexual flowers. The family includes many interesting species. Edible fruit, fibre (hemp, ramie, etc.), and timber are their principal products; some have a milky juice. From time immemorial the Fig-tree (Crann Fige) has been esteemed for its fruit. The renowned Banyan-tree of India is another species of Ficus. In hot countries the Bread-fruit is a staple article of food, the Jack-fruit, a near relative, growing to an enormous size. While Hemp (Cainb) is cultivated in temperate countries for its fibre, it is grown in India for a narcotic resin which produces intoxication. In Eastern countries the White Mulberry is planted for feeding silkworms, and the Black Mulberry (Crann Maol-Dhearc) in Europe for its fruit. The juice of the Venezuelan Cow-tree resembles milk, and is used as such by the people. Lac, dyes, etc., are obtained from other species. The India Rubber is a useful parlour plant.

Ulmus, L.

U. montana, Stokes.—Scots or Wych Elm. Leamhan. Cultivated forms, now springing up spontaneously from seed, are among the commonest trees in Kiloran woods. The wood lasts well for works in damp situations, and is locally used for cart-shafts, oars, etc.—April.

U. campestris, L., *b suberosa* (Moench).—Common Elm. Recorded by Mr Grieve.

Humulus, L.

H. Lupulus, L.—Common Hop. Lionn Luibh, C. Introduced.—July. Cultivated in Kent for the female flowers. They are dried over charcoal fires, and added to beer to give it a better flavour and stop its fermentation.

Urtica, L.

U. dioica, L.—Common Nettle. Feanndagach; Feanndag. The young tops, in spring, are used in kale (brot Feanndagaich). Boiled with oatmeal the liquid was given to cattle suffering from "tart."—Per., July.

U. pilulifera, L. — Roman Nettle. Recorded by Mr Somerville.—Ann.

U. urens, L.—Small Nettle. Feanndagach Leamhuinne. Garden weed.—Ann., August. The leaves are gathered, cut to pieces, and used as a stimulant in the food of young turkeys. W.

MYRICACEÆ (the Gale family)

A small order, some species producing wax from which candles are made. The Wax Myrtle is a hardy North American evergreen.

Myrica, L.

M. Gale, L.—Sweet Gale. Bog Myrtle. Roid(eagach). Boggy situations. An infusion of the leafy tops was given to children as a remedy for "worms."—June. It is used for numerous purposes by the Highlanders, *e.g.*, as a substitute for hops; for tanning; and from its supposed efficacy in destroying insects beds were strewn and even made of the twigs of the Gale. C. Badge of the Campbells.

CUPULIFERÆ (the Oak family)

Trees and shrubs, the inflorescence usually a more or less pendulous spike of unisexual flowers, known as a catkin. Many species grow into large trees and furnish valuable timber; the bark of some is used in tanning and also in medicine. Sweet Chestnut (Geanm-Chnò), Hazel, etc., produce edible nuts, which also yield oil. For grandeur and beauty some exotic species are unsurpassed in this country. The London Plane withstands the smoky atmosphere of London better than any other tree.

Betula, L.

A small genus of graceful trees. Various ornamental articles are made from the bark of the North American Paper-birch. Weeping forms are highly ornamental. The following were kindly named by Rev. E. S. Marshall, M.A., F.L.S.

B. alba, L.—Silver Birch. Beithe-geal. Recorded by Mr Grieve. Badge of the Clan Buchanan.

B. alba, L., × *tomentosa.*—Natural wood.—May.

B. tomentosa, Reith and Abel.—Common Birch. Beithe. This, and its varieties, constitutes the bulk of the natural woods. The wood was used of old, as now, for making bobbins. Shinties were made from the branches, as the wood was free from "deurach." Brooms and withes (gad) were made from the fine spray. The bark was used for tanning.—May.

B. tomentosa, R. and A., *b denudata,* E. S. Marshall.— South-east of Sron Fhionnlaidh.

B. tomentosa, R. and A., *c parvifolia,* E. S. M.—Dwarf trees, heather hills above Coille Bheag. Named by Mr Bennett.

Alnus, Hill.

A. rotundifolia, Mill.—Common Alder. Fèarn. Side of burn, Kiloran. It was largely employed for planting in wet situations in Kiloran woods. The bark and small branches, by boiling, gave a black dye which (with copperas) was used for dyeing yarn, etc.—March. In Ireland the wood is used for making clog-soles. The wood has the peculiarity of splitting best from the root, hence the saying : "Gach fiodh o'n bhàrr, 's am Fèarn o'n bhun." The young wood is used for making charcoal for the manufacture of gunpowder.

Corylus, L.

C. Avellana, L.—Hazel. Calltuinn. Generally used for walking-sticks, tool-handles, and in the making of agricultural and lobster creels. The nuts are edible; they were collected for burning on Hallowe'en.—March. The badge of the Colquhouns.

Quercus, L.

A numerous genus, of temperate regions. Cork is obtained from the bark of the Cork Oak, a native of South-Western Europe. The Holm or Evergreen Oak is commonly planted as an ornamental tree.

Q. Robur, L.—British Oak. Darach. Common in one or other of its forms in the eastern and southern parts of the island. In exposed positions it is seen sometimes as a prostrate, low shrub growing only to the height of the heather. The wood was locally used in house and boat building, and for the manufacture of furniture. The bark was employed for tanning the red leather that shoes were formerly made of. The mucilaginous inner bark (Failm-an-Daraich) was applied to wounds on horses.—May. Badge of the Camerons.

(?) *Q. Robur*, var. *sessiliflora*.—Coille-mhor. Specimens were, with some hesitation, named *Q. pedunculata* by several authorities.

Fagus, L.

Trees represented in gardens by pendulous forms, and others with beautiful bronze-coloured leaves.

F. sylvatica, L.—Beech. (Craobh Fàidbhile.) Growing spontaneously in dry, rocky situations with a northern exposure in Kiloran woods.—May. Beech oil is extracted from the fruit (beech-mast) in North Germany, and is used for food and for burning. The wood is hard, and valuable for planes, lasts, etc.

Salix, L.

Trees and shrubs growing in a variety of situations, both in low countries and at high alpine stations. The bark possesses febrifuge properties. Osiers for basket-making are the shoots from pollard stumps of *S. viminalis*, *S. purpurea*, *S. triandra*, etc. Willows are adapted for planting in wet situations. *S. babylonica* (Seileach-an-t-Srutha, C.), from China, is one of the best known of Weeping Willows.

S. alba, L.—White Willow. Saileóg, I. Introduced. Craobh Dhomhnuill Oig (at Seann Mhuileann), felled about thirty years ago, was of this species, and one of the largest trees in the island.—May. The wood is light and tough, and used in making cricket-bats, etc. The young wood is burned into charcoal for the manufacture of gunpowder.

S. purpurea, L.—Purple Willow. Introduced.—May.

S. viminalis, L.—Common Osier. Seileach Uisge. Near pond, Kiloran. Used for making baskets.—May.

S. stipularis, Sm.—East end of Loch Fada.—May.

S. caprea, L.—Common Sallow. Goat Willow. Plantation, Allt-ruadh. Introduced.—May. The wood and branches of the Sallow are particularly useful for making hurdles, handles of hatchets, and shoemakers' boards; its bark is bitter and astringent; the Highlanders employ it to tan leather, and the handles of various agricultural implements are made from the wood. W.

S. aurita, L.—Round-eared Willow. Sùileag, C. On heather-covered hills, often as a low shrubby plant not much taller than the heather.—May.

S. cinerea, L.—Grey Sallow. Dubh Sheileach. Common in moist situations. Used for making agricultural creels and for tanning leather. Early in the season, when the sap begins to flow and the bark parts readily from the wood, boys make whistles of the smooth branches.—May.

S. repens, L.—Creeping Willow. Seileach Làir. Found in a variety of situations at Loch Fada side and on dry sandy hills near the shore.—April.

S. repens, L., *f argentea* (Sm.).—Recorded by Mr Grieve.

[*S. Smithiana*, Willd., and *S. Smithiana*, W., var. *stipularis,* Ander.—Both from Kiloran.—May. (A.B.)]

[*S. ambigua.*—End of May. (A.B.)]

Populus, L.

A small genus of fast-growing trees. *P. nigra* is recommended for planting on stiff clays or in wet places where more valuable trees will not thrive. The Lombardy Poplar is remarkable for its slender, erect, lofty form.

P. alba, L.—White Poplar. Craobh Phobuill, C. Introduced.

P. tremula, L.—Aspen. A' Chritheach. Commonly met with in the eastern half of the island, often as stunted specimens growing out of clefts of rocks.—March. In Coille-Bheag some of the trees in favourable situations exceed thirty feet in height.

> " Ma spionas thu a' Chritheach òg
> Bidh do chridhe air chrith ri d'bheò."

P. nigra, L.—Black Poplar. Cultivated forms of this species have been planted in wet situations, and they have now attained to a considerable size, but they are liable to be blown over.

EMPETRACEÆ (the Empetrum family)

A small order of alpine, heath-like plants.

Empetrum, L.

E. nigrum, L.—Crowberry. Grainnseag; Luis na Fionnaig, C. On the east side of the island it hangs over the edges of the gullies in the natural woods. The plant was frequently applied to festering sores. The berries are said to cause headache when eaten in quantity. Grouse are fond of them ; boiled with alum they produce a dark purple dye. C. Badge of the M'Leans. Caor Fionoige, I.

Class II. MONOCOTYLEDONS

Monocotyledons comprise about a quarter of our native plants—grass-like, bulbous, or aquatic herbs. Palmaceæ is one of the most important orders, almost wholly tropical, of this class, furnishing food, housing, and utensils to the inhabitants of warm climates. Dates, coco-nuts, oil, sugar, starch, vegetable ivory, canes, etc., are among the many natural products, and mats, brooms, brushes, textile fabrics etc., manufactured articles, of this large order which find their way into commerce. To another important tropical order (Scitaminæ) belong the ginger, arrowroot, banana, plantain, manilla hemp, etc. Starchy matter from the stem of various species of palm is one of the sources of sago.

ORCHIDACEÆ (the Orchid family)

An interesting order, abundant in moist tropical forests, and comprising the loveliest flowering plants. In temperate climates they are usually terrestrial, but in the tropics many are epiphytes and grow on the stems and branches of trees. Vanilla is the dried aromatic fruit of a tall, climbing West Indian Orchid. Salep, a nutritious food, is obtained from the tubers of various terrestrial kinds. The many beautiful species introduced are grown in this country in hothouses specially built for their requirements. All the following species are perennials. They live from year to year by forming each season a new tuber beside the old one, which withers after flowering.

Malaxis, Soland

M. paludosa, Sw.—Bog Orchis. A curious little orchis found locally in the Sphagnum moss, Rioma-mhor, Machrins. —August.

Listera, Br.

L. cordata, Br.—Lesser Twayblade. A slender little plant growing out of the moss under the heather, Beinn-nan-Gudairean.—August.

L. ovata, Br.—Twayblade. Dà-Dhuilleach; Dà-Bhileach, C. Not uncommon in moist meadows.—June.

Helleborine, Hill

H. longifolia, Rendle and Britten.—Marsh Helleborine Orchis. Seen in two localities only, moist situations, sandy ground.—July.

Orchis, L.

The various species of this genus are by far the most abundant of our local orchises, adorning the landscape in early summer with their many-coloured blossoms.

O. pyramidalis, L.—Pyramidal Orchis. Shelly sandy situations. Glen and Kiloran Bay.—July.

O. mascula, L.—Early Orchis. Moth Ùrach, C. Ardskenish Glen and ledges of rocks, Druim Buiteachan.—May. Salep is prepared from the dried root of this species. The best time to gather the root is when the seed is ripe and the stalk going to fall, for then the new bulb, of which Salep is made, has arrived at its full size. They are afterwards washed, peeled, baked in an oven, and dried. It affords mild and wholesome nutriment superior to rice.—W.

O. incarnata, L.—Wet sandy situations.—June.

O. latifolia, L.—Marsh Orchis. Loch side, below Screadan.—July.

O. maculata, L.—Spotted Orchis. Ùrach Bhallach, C. Common in meadows and pastures.—June.

O. ericetorum, Linton.—Mòrag. One of the commonest species.—July.

Habenaria, Willd.

H. conopsea, Benth.—Fragrant Orchis. Lus Taghta, C. Ardskenish Glen and Balaromin-mor.—July.

H. albida, Br.—One specimen, Balanahard hills.

H. viridis, Br.—Frog Orchis. Sandy ground, Balanahard and Kiloran Bay.—July.

H. bifolia, Br.—Butterfly Orchis. A sweet-smelling species, not uncommon in moist meadows.—July.

H. virescens, Druce.—Noted by Mr Somerville in Scalasaig meadows, near the Post Office.

IRIDACEÆ (the Iris family)

Perennial herbs, usually with an enlarged root-stock—bulbs, corms, or rhizomes, etc., numerously represented in dry, sunny countries, as South Africa. The perfume, Essence of Violets, is prepared from the roots of a species of Iris. The order includes splendid flowering genera—Iris, Gladiolus, Crocus, etc.

Iris, L.

I. Pseud-acorus, L.—Yellow Iris; Yellow Flag. Seileastair. Abundant in wet situations. A grey dye is extracted, by boiling, from the root. Writing-ink was also obtained from it (with copperas). In dry situations the roots are sometimes eaten in winter by rabbits, which burrow after them into the ground.—Per., June.

AMARYLLIDACEÆ (the Amaryllis family)

Bulbous herbs, found mostly in hot, sunny countries. The bulbs are stored up with the various forms of plant-food, which enables them to tide over the dry seasons in hot climates without injury. Many species, as the Daffodil, Snowdrop (Gealag Làir), and Snowflake, have emetic and purgative properties. Some are poisonous ; the juice of a South African bulb being used by the Hottentots for poisoning their arrows. Strong fibre is obtained from species of Agave. Amaryllis are showy flowering plants of hothouses, and Narcissus, etc., of the flower-garden.

Narcissus, L.

N. Pseudo-Narcissus, L.—Daffodil ; Lent Lily. (Lus-a-Chrom-Chinn). Lus-an-Aisige, I. Introduced.—Per., April.

N. major, Curt.—Lili Bhuidhe. Introduced about a century ago, and spreading along the banks of Kiloran burn. The green leaves are minced and, mixed with their corn, given to horses for worms.—Per., April.

N. biflorus, Curt.—Primrose Peerless. Introduced, and growing in clumps at Tigh Samhraidh.—Per., May.

LILIACEÆ (the Lily family)

In this extensive order there is an interesting gathering of plants exhibiting great diversity in habit as well as in geographical distribution. Many are perennial herbs with a bulbous root-stock ; a few (Butcher's-broom) are shrubby, and some (Smilax) are climbers, while others (Dracæna, Yucca) are more or less of an arborescent character. Many possess active, sometimes poisonous, properties. Aloes is the inspissated juice of several West Indian and South African species of Aloe. The corms of the Meadow Saffron (Cròch) are used for rheumatism. The products of the order include fibre from the New Zealand and African Hemps, Sarsaparilla from the roots of Smilax, dragon's-blood from the famous Dragon-tree of Teneriffe. Liliums, Hyacinths, Tulips (Tuiliop, C.), Lily of the Valley (Lili-nan-Lòn, C.), are choice flower-

ing plants; and species of Allium, Asparagus (Creamh-mac-
Fiadh, C.), etc., indispensable kitchen-garden esculents.

Ruscus, L.

R. aculeatus, L.—Butcher's Broom.   Calg-Bhrudhainn, C.
Introduced, and useful for planting in shaded places under
trees.   In Italy it is made into besoms, with which butchers
sweep their blocks.   W.

Polygonatum, Hill.

P. officinale, All.—Solomon-seal.   A few plants grow
ing spontaneously in Kiloran woods.—Per., June.

Allium, L.

Bulbous herbs, possessing the peculiar onion or garlic smell.
The Onion (Uinnean) is believed to have originated in Africa.
It was cultivated in ancient times by the Egyptians and
the Jews.   The Leek (Creamh-Gàraidh) is now regarded as
a cultivated variety of the Wild Leek.   The Shallot (Sgalaid,
C.) and the Garlic (Gairgean Gàraidh) are other useful species.

A. Schœnoprasum, L.—Chives.   Feuran.   Cultivated in
gardens for the leaves, which are used as a spring seasoning
for soups, mashed potatoes, etc.

A. ursinum, L.—Ramsons; Broad-leaved Garlic.   Creamh.
Common in damp situations in Kiloran woods, and in gullies
along the northern shore.   Formerly used for seasoning.   It
is said to impart a disagreeable flavour to the milk of cows
and to the flesh of rabbits that eat it.—Per., June.

Scilla, L.

S. verna, Huds.—Spring Squill.   Lear-Uinnean, C.
Not rare in sandy, rocky situations at the shore.   White
forms of it were seen at Poll Gorm.—Per., May.

S. non-scripta, Hoffmgg. and Link. — Wood Hyacinth;

English Bluebell. Bogha-Muc. Abundant, Kiloran woods, where white forms are not uncommon.—Per., May. This plant was not liked by the ancients because they believed it grew from the blood of Hyakinthos, a youth killed by Apollo with a quoit when in one of his mad fits; hence the name. W.

Narthecium, Huds.

N. ossifragum, Huds.—Bog Asphodel. (Bliochan.) Badly-drained, marshy situations.—Per., July. Luibh Chalum Chille, by which it is known by some persons locally, is more correctly applied to *Hypericum pulchrum* (Slender St John's Wort).

JUNCACEÆ (the Rush family)

Plants with stiff, grass-like leaves and inconspicuous dry flowers, found in all parts of the world. Some species furnish material for mats, baskets, etc. They constitute a good deal of the rough herbage of the island. All of the following but the Toad Rush are perennials.

Juncus, L.

The principal genus of the order, usually found growing in badly drained and marshy situations.

J. bufonius, L.—Toad Rush. The only British annual Rush ; common in muddy places.—July.

J. squarrosus, L.—Heath Rush. Tarruing-air-eigin ; Tarruing-gun-taing ; Bru-chorpan. Common on moors and hill pastures ; usually found growing in drier situations than most Rushes.—June.

J. compressus, Jacq.—Recorded by Mr Grieve.

J. Gerardi, Lois.—Abundant at Port Mor, Strand, etc.— June.

J. effusus, L.—Soft Rush. Edge of marshy ground below Carnan Eoin.

J. conglomeratus, L.—Common Rush. Luachair.

Abundant in wet situations on the low ground. The characters that are used for distinguishing between this and the preceding species are not constant, and the two are often found to merge into one another. The pith was used for the old-fashioned rush-lights, the oil being obtained from the liver of saiths (coal-fish). The pith was collected beforehand, and hung up in the houses to dry.—July.

J. bulbosus, L.—Along the shallow margins of Loch Fada and in other wet situations, often exhibiting considerable diversity in form and in shade of colour, from light green to dark brown.—July.

J. bulbosus, var. *fluitans*.—Loch Fada, in deeper water than the preceding.

J. subnodulosus, Schrank.—Abundant at Aird, Machrins. This kind was locally regarded as being superior to the commoner kind (*J. sylvaticus*) for thatching, as it is harder and lasts better.—August.

J. articulatus, L.—Jointed Rush. Kiloran Bay sands.

J. sylvaticus, Reich.—Sharp-flowered Jointed Rush. Frafann. The common species, abundant in meadows and wet situations. It is largely used for thatching, as it lasts longer than the Common Rush.—July.

Luzula, DC.

Perennial herbs with flat, grass-like leaves growing in drier situations than the Rushes.

L. pilosa, Willd.—Hairy Woodrush. Kiloran woods.—May.

L. sylvatica, Gaud.—Great Woodrush. Seileastair-nan-Gobhar; Aineach. Abundant on rocky ledges and slopes with a northern exposure. It is sometimes eaten by rabbits in winter.—May.

L. compestris, DC.—Field Rush. Common in dry pastures.—May.

L. multiflora, DC.—Leana Ghlas; not uncommon.—May.

L. multiflora, *b congesta* (Lej.).—Goirtean Artair, Leana Ghlas.—June.

TYPHACEÆ (the Reedmace family)

The local representatives of the order are aquatic perennials with long, linear leaves. The leaves of the Bull-rush (Bog-Sheimhin, I.) are used for making chair-bottoms, mats, etc.

Sparganium, L.

S. erectum, L.—Branched Bur-reed. Seasg Righ, C. Ditch, roadside between Post Office and Hotel. Common.—July.

S. minimum, Fr.—Small Bur-reed. Kiloran .burn; frequent in pools.—July.

LEMNACEÆ (the Duckweed family)

Floating herbs, consisting of small leaf-like fronds which send out delicate root-like fibres into the water beneath.

Lemna, L.

L. minor, L.—Lesser Duckweed. (Lus-gun-Mhàthair-gun-Athair.) On still pools south of Port Mor.—Per., June. The Lemnæ generally are considered to possess the property of purifying the unwholesome air in marshy places. Ducks and geese are fond of all the species. W.

ALISMACEÆ (the Alisma family)

A small group of marsh or aquatic species. The Flowering Rush, Arrowhead, and Water Plantain, British species, are suitable for planting at the margins of ornamental waters.

Alisma, L.

A. ranunculoides, L.—The Lesser Water Plantain. (Corr-Chopag.) Frequent in marshy situations.—Per., June.

NAIADACEÆ (the Naiad family)

An order of marsh or aquatic plants, some with floating leaves, others entirely submerged in deep water, occurring in the sea as well as in fresh waters. All the following are perennials.

Triglochin, L.

T. palustre, L. — Arrow-grass. Bàrr-a-Mhilltich, C. Boggy and marshy places.—June. Cows are extremely fond of it. W.

T. maritimum, L.—Sea Arrow-grass. Not uncommon in the salt-marshes.—May.

Potamogeton, L.

A considerable genus, difficult to determine, and abundantly represented throughout the island. The plants in the following list were identified by Mr Arthur Bennett, F.L.S.

P. natans, L.—Broad Pondweed. Kiloran burn. Common. —July.

P. polygonifolius, Pourr.—Oblong Pondweed. Duilleaga-bàite. The common kind abundant in running and in stagnant waters, deep and shallow. The leaves were applied to scalding burns for cooling. Also used as an ingredient in certain plasters. Duilleaga-bàite-firionn were credited with greater healing properties than other kinds, but the species to which the name applied was not discovered.—July.

P. polygonifolius, var. *pseudo-fluitans*.—Marsh ; head of the Glen.

P. Gessnaceasis, Fischer.—Pool of brackish water, Rudha Gheadha. This is a hybrid between *P. natans*, L., and *P. polygonifolius*, Pourr., and occurs in Ireland (A. B.).

P. alpinus, Balb.—Burn, Geadhail-na-Crithe.—June.

P. heterophyllus, Schreb. — Various-leaved Pondweed. West Loch Fada and Loch Colla.—July.

P. heterophyllus, c graminifolius (Fr.).—Loch Sgoltaire.—August.

P. nitens, Weber.—West Loch Fada.—July.

P. perfoliatus, L.—West Loch Fada.—July.

P. pusillus, L.—Slender Pondweed. West Loch Fada; common.—July.

P. pusillus, b tenuissimus, Koch.—Middle Loch Fada. (A later examination of specimens leads Mr Bennett to hope that this may turn out to be *P. trichoides*, Cham.)

P. Sturrockii, Ar. Benn.—Loch Sgoltaire and Loch Fada.

P. pectinatus, L.—Fennel Pondweed. Pools, western shores.—August.

P. filiformis, Nolte.—Pools, western shores.

Ruppia, L.

R. maritima, L.—Shore pool, Poll Gorm.—July.

R. rostellata, Koch. — Tassel Pondweed. Shore pools, south of Port Mor.—June.

Zannichellia, L.

Z. palustris, L. — Horned Pondweed. Shore pools, Machrins.—August.

Zostera, L.

Z. marina, L. — Grasswrack. Bilearach. Abundant, growing where sediment has been deposited in the sea, and frequently washed ashore.—July. The long, grass-like leaves, when dried, are used for packing, and for stuffing mattresses. W.

Naias, L.

N. flexilis, Rostk. and Schmidt.—Slender Naiad. Found in the three divisions of Loch Fada.—August. "A very interesting find. For many years it was only on record from Ireland; then my late friend Abram Sturrock found it in East Perth, and Dr White in Mid Perth. It is rare in

Europe, occurring only in Pomerania, Finland, and Upland, and Scania in Sweden " (A. B.).

CYPERACEÆ (the Sedge family)

Grass-like herbs, usually found in moist situations and at the edges of waters. The leaves are usually stiffer than those of grasses; the stems are solid, and the sheaths of the leaves closed all round. All the species of the order included here are perennials.

Eleocharis, Br.

E. palustris, Roem. and Schult. — Creeping Club-rush. Ditch, Garvard; common.—July.

E. uniglumus, Schultes. — One-glumed Spike-rush. Marshy ground above Loch Sgoltaire.—August.

E. multicaulis, Sm.—Many-stalked Club-rush. In tufts on stony shore, Loch Fada side.—July.

Scirpus, L.

S. pauciflorus, Lightf. — Few-flowered Club-rush. Elevated moorland between Kilchattan and Machrins.—August.

S. cæspitosus, L.—Tufted Club-rush; Deer's Hair. Ciob. Abundant on the moors, often mixed with the heather. It is particularly common in places on the grits.—June. This is the principal food of cattle and sheep in the Highlands in March and till the end of May. W. Locally it is not often eaten by sheep.

S. fluitans, L.—Floating Club-rush. Common in streams and in marshy pools of still water.—August.

S. filiformis, Savi.—A slender and elegant species, seen only at a muddy corner of Leana-mhor, Garvard.—August.

S. setaceus, L.—Bristle Club-rush. Common in moist places in the hill pastures.—July.

S. lacustris, L. — Lake Club-rush. Luachair Bhogain.

Margins of Loch Fada.—July. It was formerly used in making horse-collars, baskets, etc., in various parts of the country.

S. maritimus, L.—Sea Club-rush. Seasg-na-Mara. Common in salt-marshes.—August. Cows eat it ; the roots, dried and ground to powder, have been used instead of flour in times of scarcity. W.

S. rufus, Schrad.—Plentiful in the salt-marshes at Port Mor and the Strand.—May and June.

Eriophorum, L.

E. vaginatum, L.—Hare's-tail Cotton-grass. Canach-ant-Sléibh. Usually growing more in tufts and flowering rather earlier than the following species, often at higher elevations.—May.

E. angustifolium, Roth.—Common Cotton - grass. An Canach. Abundant in boggy places. The cottony tufts were gathered and used for stuffing pillows and cushions.—June.

> "S'e bu leaba dhuinn an Luachair
> S'e bu chluasag dhuinn an Canach."

This plant is useful in the island of Skye to support cattle in the earlier part of spring, before other grasses are sufficiently grown. Pennant's *Tour*, 1774.

E. angustifolium, b. minus, Koch.—Marshy ground, Carnan Eoin, at an elevation of 400 feet.

E. angustifolium, d. elatius, Koch.—Boggy ground, burnside, Leana Ghlas.—July.

Schœnus, L.

S. nigricans, L.—Bog-rush. Sèimhean C. Frequent in wet hollows through which the surrounding water drains.—June.

S. nigricans, f nanus.—Northern slopes of Beinn-a-Sgoltaire.—June.

Cladium, P. Br.

C. Mariscus, Br.—Great Twig-rush. Colgróc, I. Growing at the edges of the lochs.—August.

Carex, L.

A large genus constituting an important part of the herbage of the meadows and hilly pastures of the island. With careful drainage they are displaced by the more nutritious grasses.

C. dioica, L.—Ill-drained, spongy ground.—May.

C. pulicaris, L. — Flea Sedge. Wet situation, Baile Mhaide ; not uncommon.—June.

C. arenaria, L.—Sea Sedge ; Sea Matgrass. Tàithean. A common plant of the blown sands, and one that greatly assists in binding them. The long, creeping roots were made into cattle-ties. In former times, when cattle were ferried across to the mainland on their way to the markets of the south, it was part of every cattleman's duty to have a certain number of these ties prepared beforehand.—June.

C. vulpina, L.—Fox Sedge. At the seaside, Port Mor and other places.—June.

C. echinata, Murr.—Little Prickly Sedge. Interstices in rocks, Port Olmsa, and shore turf, Port-an-Obain, Balanahard, etc.—June.

C. remota, L.—Damp gully near shore, south of Rudha Gheadha ; rare.—June.

C. leporina, L.—Oval-spiked Sedge. Rather common in moist situations in pastures.—June. (*C. ovalis*, Good.— A. B.).

C. Goodenowii, Gay.—In one or other of its forms the commonest sedge in the island. Frequently found growing in comparatively dry situations on the hill-sides as well as in thoroughly marshy low-lying situations. The most variable of local species, it is also one of the earliest to start into growth, often enticing cattle when other food is scarce into dangerously boggy places where they are sometimes lost.— June.

C. Goodenowii, Gay, *b juncella* (Fr.).—Wet ground, sea-side, Port-an-Tigh-Mhoir.—June.

C. Goodenowii, Gay, *tornata*, Fr.—Peat-bogs, Riskbuie.— June.

C. flacca, Schreb.—Growing in large patches, meadows, Riskbuie. One of the commonest Sedges. Patches of badly drained land are often plainly indicated by the presence in quantity of this glaucous green-foliaged plant. A very vari-able species. (*C. glauca*.—A. B.).—June.

C. limosa, L.—Mud Sedge. Alluvium flats near Loch Colla, and at Lochan-a-Bhràghad.—June and July.

C. pilulifera, L.—Pill-headed Sedge. Crevices in rocks above Teampull-a-Ghlinne.—May.

C. caryophyllea, Latourr.—Vernal Sedge. Kiloran Bay, and turf, Port-an-Obain, Scalasaig.—May and June.

C. pallescens, L.—Pale Sedge. Damp hollow, Coille-mhor natural wood.—June.

C. panicea, L.—Pink-leaved Sedge. Not uncommon in moist meadows.—June.

C. panicea, *b. tumidula*, Laestad.—Damp pasture, seaside, north of Port Mor.—June. "A very interesting form found also in Ross" (A. B.).

C. sylvatica, Huds. — Wood Sedge. Coille-mhor and Kiloran woods.—June. The Laplanders prepare a coarse clothing from this plant. Linn.

C. helodes, Link.—Smooth-stalked Beaked Sedge. Grow-ing from interstices in rocks above Lochan-a-Raonabuilg (*C. lævigata*, Sm. A. B.).

C. binervis, Sm.—One of the commonest Sedges, and found growing in a variety of situations, often in tuft-like masses. It is found both at high-water mark and growing on the summits of the hills, and is one of the first plants to start into growth where the heather has been burned. It is also one of the first to become established where the heath-covered turf has been removed.—June.

C. distans, L.—Distant Sedge. Shore rocks above Port Mor and Traigh-nam-Bàrc Bay.—June and July.

C. fulva, Host.—Uncultivated hillocks, Gàradh Gainmhich, in moist situations ; not uncommon.—June.

C. extensa, Good.—Shore rocks, Balaromin-mor.—July.

C. extensa, *b pumila*, And.—Shore rocks at high-water mark, Rudha Gheadha.—June.

C. flava, L.—Yellow Sedge. Damp pasture, Kiloran.— June.

C. Œderi, Retz.—Wet ground near Loch Colla, and moist hollow, east coast.—June.

C. Œderi, *c. cyperoides*, Marss.—Recorded by Mr Somerville.

C. lasiocarpa, Ehrh.—Slender Sedge. Edge of Loch-na-Sgùid, and marshy ground, Loch Colla.—May.

C. hirta, L.—Hairy Sedge. Moist meadow below Balaromin-mor farm-house.—July.

C. inflata, Huds.—Bottle Sedge. Seasg-uisge. Abundant in the shallow water at the edge of Loch Fada. Used for thatching, and lasting well.—June. (*C. ampullacea*, Good. —A. B.).

GRAMINEAE (the Grass family)

One of the largest and most important of the natural orders of plants. In Britain all the species are herbs, but in the tropics some kinds (Bamboos = Cuilc Fhrangach) grow to the height of tall trees. As forming the chief supply of food for man and forage for animals, Rice (Rìs), Indian Corn (Coirce-mor), Millets (Muileud, I.), Wheat (Cruithneachd), Oats (Coirce), Barley (Eorna), Rye (Seagal), are cultivated in all parts of the world. Rye Grasses and other kinds are extensively grown as forage plants (fodar),

Sugar (Siucar) is obtained from the sweet sap of various species. The Sugar Cane—for its sugar, rum, molasses—is an important crop of hot climates. Other products of the order are aromatic oils, ornamental seeds (Job's Tears), straw for plaiting and thatching. Macaroni and vermicelli are prepared in Italy and Sicily from fine wheat-flour; "corn-flour" is obtained from Indian Corn. Bamboos are put to an endless variety of uses; a hardy kind (Metake) thrives locally. The Pampas Grass and Provence Reed make handsome specimens for lawns, and many smaller kinds—Feather Grass, Quaking Grass, Agrostis—are used for decorative purposes.

Phalaris, L.

A small genus, including the Canary Grass, from which the canary seed is obtained, now appearing in the country as a weed of cultivation.

P. arundinacea, L.—Reed Canary Grass. Not uncommon at sides of ditches.—Per., July. The Gardeners' Garters or Ribbon Grass often seen in gardens is a variegated form.

Anthoxanthum, L.

A. odoratum, L.—Sweet Vernal Grass. (Mislean.) Abundant in well-drained situations.—Per., May. It imparts the characteristic sweet scent to new-mown hay, and is a valuable ingredient in pastures on account of its early growth and for continuing to send up leaves until late in the autumn. With the exception, perhaps, of sheep, domestic animals show no great partiality for it, but where it is abundant it is said to improve the quality of mutton.

Alopecurus, L.

A. geniculatus, L. — Marsh Foxtail. Fìdeag Cham, C. Not uncommon in marshy meadows.—Per., July.

A. pratensis, L.—Meadow Foxtail. (Fìdeag.) Kiloran

meadows.—Per., June. One of the best of forage grasses, and well adapted for moist land. It constitutes the greater portion of many of the richer natural pastures of Britain.

Phleum, L.

P. pratense, L.—Timothy; Cat's-tail. (Bodan.) Kiloran meadows.—Per., July. An excellent forage plant of which all animals are fond, and a valuable ingredient of pastures. It was introdnced from America as a forage crop about 1761, and it was first known as Timothy in South Carolina, having been taken to that State by a Mr Timothy Hansom. It thrives on heavy soils and those of a peaty nature.

Agrostis, L.

A. canina, L.—Brown Bent-grass. Commons and moors.—Per., July.

A. alba, L.—Marsh Bent-grass. Feorine, C. Abundant in marshy situations. One of the commonest grasses.—Per., August.

A. alba, b. stolonifera (L.).—Fiorin-grass. Bushy ground, Kiloran.—Per., July and August. Recommended for moist soils and irrigated meadows. It affords herbage early in spring and late in autumn.

A. alba, c. maritima, Meyer.—Edge of shore pools, Port Mor; not uncommon in such situations.—July.

A. tenuis, Sibth.—Fine Bent-grass. Well-drained pasture, Screadan. — Per., July. A suitable species for dry soils; and although cattle are not fond it, sheep are said to relish it, particularly in winter. It will grow on bare, exposed places where more valuable kinds fail.

A. tenuis, var. *pumila*.—Growing in very dwarf tufts on bare, rocky sands, Cul-Salach.—July.

A. nigra, With.—Garvard.—August.

Ammophila, Host.

A. arenaria, Link. — Sea Maram ; Matweed. Muran. Planted locally on the blown sands to prevent them shifting. One of the best and most lasting materials used locally for thatching houses.—Per., August. It is recorded that mat and rope making from this species was the only handicraft of the inhabitants of the village of Newborough in Wales about the beginning of the seventeenth century.

Aira, L.

A. caryophyllea, L.—Silvery Hair-grass. Sandy pasture, upper part of Gàradh Gainmhich.—Ann., June.

A. præcox, L. — Early Hair-grass. Common in rather bare rocky places on the hills.—Ann., May. This and the preceding species are soon dried up, and can yield nothing but a little early food for sheep. W.

Deschampsia, Beauv.

D. cæspitosa, Beauv.—Tufted Hair-grass. Cuiseag Airgid(?). Growing in large tufts or tussocks in wet situations, enabling the collector to pass dry-shod over wet and boggy places. The highly ornamental flowering panicles are used for winter decoration. Its very coarse herbage is seldom eaten by animals.—Per., July.

D. flexuosa, Trin.—Waved Hair-grass. Moin-fheur, C. Frequent in rough pastures and meadows, often on peaty soils.—Per., July. The seed of this species is often substituted for the more valuable Yellow Oat-grass.

D. flexuosa, b. montana, Hook. fil. — A pretty, purplish-coloured form not uncommon on the hills.—July.

Holcus, L.

H. mollis, L. — Soft Meadow-grass. Woods, Kiloran ; local.—Per., July. Not unsuitable for sowing in wooded or barren places; and its creeping roots render it useful for binding dry, sandy slopes.

H. lanatus, L.—Yorkshire Fog; Woolly Soft Grass. Common on impoverished soils.—Per., July. It should be regarded as a weed rather than a proper ingredient of pastures, and every means used for its extirpation. Stock are not fond of it either in the green state or dried as hay ; the latter being spongy and unfit for horses.

Avena, L.

Cultivated varieties of Oat have sprung from *A. sativa* (the Common Oat). The Yellow Oat (*A. flavescens*, L.) is a desirable constituent in pastures and meadows, being valuable both for grazing and hay.

A. pubescens, Huds.—Downy Oat-grass. In the vicinity of the limestone rock, Uragaig. A lime-loving plant, producing but scanty herbage.—Per., June.

A. pratensis, L.—Perennial Oat. Coirce Fiadhain, C. Recorded by Mr Grieve.

Arrhenatherum, Beauv.

A. elatius, Mert. and Koch.—False Oat-grass. Kiloran meadows.—Per., July. The herbage is said to be bitter and not much relished by cattle. It will grow in shaded woods and plantations.

A. elatius, b bulbosum, Presl.—Goin-Fheur. A weed of sandy fields, with knotted roots which, in winter time, are burrowed for and eaten by rabbits.

Sieglingia, Bernh.

S. decumbens, Bernh.—Decumbent Heath-grass. Hilly pastures, Dun Ghaillionn.—Per., July.

Phragmites, Adans.

P. communis, Trin.—Common Reed. Cuilc. Abundant at the edges of the lochs and sometimes used for thatching. Per., August. The plumes are useful for winter decoration, and in France and Italy they are made into dusting-brushes.

Cynosurus, L.

C. cristatus, L. — Crested Dog's-tail. Coin-Fheur, I. Dry pastures.—Per., June. As it sends up many leaves from the base, it is recommended for lawns which are frequently cut. It forms a close turf, and sheep are said to be less subject to foot-rot in pastures where it grows.

Kœleria, Pers.

K. gracilis, Pers.—Shore rocks, Port Mor ; not uncommon on dry banks.—Per., June. Produces but little foliage, which is covered with short, downy hairs.

Molinia, Schrank.

M. cœrulea, Moench. — Purple Melic-grass. Bràbàn, I. Although very abundant in wet meadows and badly drained hill pastures, all kinds of stock reject it if they can get other food. When compelled to take too much of it in hay, they are liable to get into a bad condition.—Per., August.

Catabrosa, Beauv.

C. aquatica, Beauv. — Water Whorl - grass. At the mouths of freshwater streams on the seashore.—July.

C. aquatica, b. littoralis, Parn.—Mouth of small stream, Kiloran Bay sands.— August.

Dactylis, L.

A genus of a single species. An elegant variegated form is used for edgings in gardens.

D. glomerata, L.—Rough Cock's-foot Grass. Common.—
Per., July. Remarkable for the rapidity of its growth, it
yields an enormous crop of nutritious herbage, growing well
in shady, well-drained situations.

Briza, L.

B. media, L. — Quaking-grass. Crith Fheur. Kiloran
meadows. — Per., June. Prized as a decorative grass.
Generally found on impoverished soils, and dying out under
good cultivation.

Poa, L.

A large genus, including valuable fodder plants. The
Alpine Meadow - grass (*P. alpina*) thrives at elevations
where scarcely any other pasture plant will grow.

P. annua, L.—Annual Poa. The commonest British
plant, forming the chief ingredient of the grass in the
London parks. Flowers all the year round.—Ann.

P. nemoralis, L. — Wood Meadow-grass. Local.—Per.,
July. Of very early growth and suitable for lawns and
ornamental grounds in places shaded with trees.

P. pratensis, L. — Smooth-stalked Meadow-grass. In
rather dry, rocky situations, producing an early herbage.
—Per., June.

P. trivialis, L.—Rough-stalked Meadow-grass.—Common
Per., July. In wet, dry, or shaded situations. A valuable
and highly nutritious grass for low-lying pastures.

Glyceria, Br.

G. fluitans, Br.—Manna Grass; Floating Sweet Grass.
Cuiseag Mhilis. Milsean Uisge, C. Sluggish streams and
stagnant waters. The plant was formerly well known to
children for the honey contained in the flowers.—Per., July.
All grazing animals are fond of it, and the seeds are greedily
eaten by marsh - fowl and freshwater fish — trout, etc.

Semolina was formerly prepared from them. The seeds are small, but very sweet and nourishing. They are collected in several parts of Germany and Poland, and are esteemed as a delicacy in soups and gruels. When ground to meal they make bread very little inferior to that made from wheat. W.

G. fluitans, b. triticea, Fr.—Damp hollow, Fang.—July.

G. plicata, Fr.—Shallow, stagnant pool in meadow, Bala-romin-mor.—July.

G. maritima, Mert. and Koch.—Creeping Sea Meadow-grass. Shore rocks and shore turf, Port Mor.—June.

Festuca, L.

A widely distributed genus of temperate climates, including some of our most valuable pasture grasses. *F. pratensis* (Meadow Fescue) is excellent for permanent pasture. It forms a considerable portion of the herbage of the natural pastures on the mainland.

F. rottboellioides, Kunth.—Sea Hard-grass. Pier wall and dry sandy situations along the southern shore.—Ann., June.

F. bromoides, L.—Sandy ground, upper part of Druim-buidhe, and cultivated fields, Machrins.—Ann., June. (*F. scuiroides.*—A. B.).

F. ovina, L. — Sheep's Fescue. Feur Chaorach, C. This grass constitutes one of the principal ingredients in the herbage of the dry hill pastures.—Per., June. It forms a large proportion of the sheep pastures of the Highlands; its presence indicating dry conditions, and the consequent adaptability of such situations for sheep.

F. rubra, L.—Creeping Fescue. Top of rocks, Port-an-Obain, Balanahard. Common on the sea rocks, and suitable for sowing on dry, sandy soils.—Per., July.

F. rubra, g. arenaria, Fr.—Recorded by Mr Somerville.

F. elatior, L.—Tall Fescue. Side of Port Lobh burn, Machrins, and gully below Uragaig.—Per., July. Notwithstanding its coarseness, cattle are fond of it, and it is recommended for sowing in permanent pastures. It grows to a height of 3 to 4 feet.

Bromus, L.

B. ramosus, Huds.—Smooth Brome-grass. Gully below Tigh Iain Daraich.—Per., August.

B. commutatus, Schrad.—One plant, roadside, Kiloran.—Bi., June.

B. hordeaceus, L.—Soft Brome. Frequently met with in Kiloran. Of small value for pastures.—July.

Brachypodium, Beauv.

B. sylvaticum, Roem. and Schult.—Slender False Brome. Shady situation on large boulders, mouth of New Cave.—Per., July. "It is not liked by domesticated animals, but deer and rabbits eat it."

Lolium, L.

L. perenne, L. — Perennial Ryegrass. Breoillean, C. Common at the edges of fields.—Per., June. Extensively cultivated as a forage plant, and cultivated in England for this purpose as early as 1677. It is suitable for a great variety of soils, and adapted in an eminent degree for alternate husbandry, producing a large bulk of highly nutritious herbage.

L. perenne, *c multiflorum* (Lam.). — Italian Rye-grass. A garden weed, Kiloran.—June. It was introduced as a forage grass from Hamburg in 1831, and from Italy in 1833. As it is biennial in its nature, this species is more suited for alternate husbandry than for permanent pastures. It grows quickly and luxuriantly, and cattle are very fond of it. The seed that is imported is said to yield an earlier and a heavier crop than what is ripened in this country.

Agropyron, J. Gaertn.

A. *caninum*, Beauv.—Bearded Wheat-grass. Growing up through hedge, roadside, Cnoc-an-Arbhair. It shoots out its bright green leaves early in spring.—Per., July.

A. *repens*, Beauv.—Quitch-grass; Couch-grass. Feur-a-Phuint, C. Troublesome weed.—Per., July.

A. *junceum*, Beauv.—Shore-wheat. Glas Fheur, C. Edge of sand-banks, Kiloran Bay, and sandy bay, Meall-a-Chuilbh. —Per., August.

Lepturus, Br.

L. *filiformis*, Trin.—Rather a rare British plant of maritime sands, recorded by Mr Grieve.

Nardus, L.

N. *stricta*, L.—Common Nard; Heath Matgrass. Beitean ; Borrach, C. One of the commonest moor grasses. It is wiry, and animals are not fond of it.—Per., June.

Div. II. *GYMNOSPERMS*

Gymnosperms do not, like the Angiosperms, have their ovules enclosed in a seed-vessel (ovary), but develop them directly upon the axis, as in the Yew, or upon capillary leaves, as in the cones of the Pine, Fir, Larch, etc. They are fertilised by the pollen-grains falling directly upon them. Gymnosperms form a connecting link between the Angiosperms and the higher Cryptogams.

CONIFERÆ (the Pine family)

An extensive order, including many excellent timber trees which also yield resins (pitch, turpentine, tar) and aromatic oils and balsams with medicinal properties. Some—Yew (Iubhar), Cypress (Sipreis ; Craobh Bhròin) — possess poisonous qualities. Vast forests of conifers alone are to be met with in the Northern Hemisphere. The Mammoth Tree of California attains a height of upwards of 400 feet; the Redwood, a close ally, also growing to a great size. The Yellow Pine (Giubhas Buidhe), Pitch Pine (G. Dearg), White Pine (G. Geal), etc., are highly valued for building purposes. Large plantations of Larch (Learag), Fir, Spruce, etc., have been made in this country. Cedar (Seudar), Cypress, Juniper, and other ornamental species are commonly planted in pleasure-grounds. Conifers generally do not thrive in the smoky atmosphere of towns, nor, unless well screened, in close proximity to the sea.

Juniperus, L.

A numerous genus of evergreen shrubs or small trees. The aromatic wood of the American Red Cedar is used in cabinet-making and for lead-pencils.

J. communis, L.—Common Juniper. Iubhar Beinne. Frequently prostrate and spreading, sometimes to the length of three or four yards. Dead remains of stems much larger than those now growing are to be seen. The green branches were burned for fumigating houses after infectious diseases. The berries, which take two years to come to maturity, were used for flavouring whisky, as they still are in other countries for flavouring gin.—May. They are diuretic, and yield an oil of medicinal value.

J. communis, b. intermedia, Nyman.—Balanahard hills.

J. sibirica, Burgsdorf.—Rocky hillocks, Poll Gorm and southern end of Ardskenish, in exposed situations.—May.

Pinus, L.

Though constituting the bulk of the Coniferæ in the Northern Hemisphere, this genus is unknown in the southern half of the globe. Austrian, Corsican, Himalayan, and Stone Pines are among those that are commonly planted. The

Cluster and Sea Pines have been planted with success on bare sand-hills of maritime districts in France.

P. sylvestris, L. — Norway or Riga Pine; Scots Fir. Giubhas. Introduced; one seedling was found growing in Druim Buiteachan under natural conditions, but the seedlings are probably eaten as they grow by rabbits.—May. This species yields Burgundy pitch. The badge of the Clan M'Gregor (Clan Alpin).

P. Pinaster, Ait.—Cluster Pine. Introduced.

CRYPTOGAMS OR FLOWERLESS PLANTS

Although the members of this group have sexual organs they do not bear flowers with stamens and pistils. Reproduction is brought about by minute cellular bodies called spores. These are produced in abundance, in special structures, on the underside of the fronds of Ferns, in the axils of the leaves of Selaginella, etc. Cryptogams comprise the simplest forms of plant life. They are conveniently divided into two series —Vascular and Cellular. In the former (Ferns, etc.) there is a manifest distinction, as in flowering plants, between stem and leaf, and their tissues include vascular as well as cellular elements; in the latter (Moulds, Algæ, etc.), no such distinction between stem and leaf exists, their structure being simply cellular.

FILICES (the Fern family)

This is by far the most important group of the Vascular Cryptogams, found in abundance in all moist climates. In warm countries some species (Tree-ferns) are arborescent in character; others are climbers. A few possess active properties. Adiantums (Maiden-hair), Pteris, Asplenium, etc., are largely grown in hothouses for their elegant foliage. The Parsley and Oak (Sgeamh Dharaich, C.) Ferns occur in the Northern Islands, and the Adder's-tongue (Lus-na-

Nathrach, C.) in the Outer Hebrides. All the local species
have a perennial root-stock.

Hymenophyllum, Sm.

H. tunbridgense, Sm.—Filmy Fern. Rocky mossy banks
with a northern exposure ; natural woods and plantations,
Kiloran.

H. peltatum, Desv.—Recorded by Mr Grieve.

Pteris, L.

P. aquilina, L.—Brake ; Bracken. ((F)raineach(mhor).)
Abundant in woods and pastures in well-drained situations.
On the exposed hill-tops it is scarcely a foot in height, but
in the sheltered gullies on the East Coast it grows to 7 or 8
feet. It is spreading rapidly and monopolising a good deal
of the best of the ground. It is cut and stacked for winter
bedding for cattle. Meal is prepared from the thick fleshy
roots (rhizomes) in Japan, where the young shoots are also
said to be eaten like asparagus. In Monmouthshire the
green tops were burned in the summer time and the ashes
moulded into balls for washing, before washing soda came
into such general use.

Blechnum, L.

B. Spicant, With.—Hard Fern. ((F)raineach Chruaidh.)
Abundant in hilly pastures, under banks, and on rocky slopes
facing the north.

Asplenium, L.

A. Adiantum-nigrum, L. — Black Spleenwort. (An
Raineach-uaine.) Commonly growing out of crevices and
joints in rocks in shady situations.

A. marinum, L.—Sea Spleenwort. ((F)raineach-na-Mara.)
Abundantly growing out of interstices in the sea rocks on
the East Coast, sometimes down to high-water mark.

A. Trichomanes, L.—Maiden-hair Spleenwort.—Dubh

Chasach; Lus na Seilg, C. Boiled in milk and strained, it was considered a good remedy for coughs and chest ailments. The species is now much more plentiful than it was when regularly collected for medicinal purposes.

A. Ruta-muraria, L.—Wall Rue. (Rue Bhallaidh, C.) Not uncommon on old walls.

Athyrium, Roth.

A. Filix-fœmina, Roth.—Lady Fern. Frith-Raineach. Raineach Mhuire, C. Abundant. Frith-Raineach is often indiscriminately applied locally to this and various species of Lastræas.

Phyllitis, Hill.

P. Scolopendrium, Newm.—Hart's-tongue Fern. Teang'-an-Fhéidh. Not uncommon in the rocky gullies of the northern shore and in the vicinity of Kiloran. An infusion of the leaves was used as a remedy for coughs and colds.

Cystopteris, Bernh.

C. fragilis, Bernh. — Brittle Bladderfern. Friodh Raineach, C. Recorded from the neighbourhood of the New Cave by Messrs Grieve and Miller.

Polystichum, Roth.

P. aculeatum, Roth.—Prickly Shield Fern. Ibhig, C. An evergreen fern frequently found in the vicinity of the New Cave.

P. aculeatum, b lobatum (Presl.).—Rocky slopes facing the north, Driseig.—September.

P. angulare, Presl.—Soft Prickly Shield Fern. A few plants. Confirmed by Mr C. Druery, F.L.S. Not previously recorded from the Western Isles, though at one time occurring in Arran and adjacent islets. In 1899 plants were discovered by the late Mr Somerville in the woods at Skipness in the Kintyre peninsula. The species is not known to have occurred on the mainland north of the Forth and Clyde. South of that line, though by no means common, it has been found in a number of counties, and it is not rare in either England or Ireland.

Lastrœa, Presl.

L. montana, T. Moore.—Mountain Shield Fern. Crim-Raineach, C. Shady gully, Coille-mhor; not uncommon.

L. Filix-mas, Presl.—Male Fern. Marc-Raineach, C. Abundant in woods, and often in sunny positions along the banks of streams. In sheltered situations it remains green through the winter. " Its root-stock is used in medicine as a remedy for tape-worm."

L. spinulosa, Presl. — Prickly-toothed Buckler Fern. Abundant on mossy and rocky banks facing the north.

L. aristata, Rendle and Britten.—Broad Buckler Fern. Common in Kiloran woods.

L. œmula, Brackenridge.—Recorded by Mr Grieve.

Polypodium, L.

P. vulgare, L.—Common Polypody. (Ceis-Chrann.) On old walls and on the mossy trunks of trees.

Phegopteris, Presl.

P. polypodioides, Fée.—Beech Fern. Moist slopes facing the north, Druim Buiteachan and other places.

Osmunda, L.

O. regalis, L.—Royal Fern. Righ Raineach. Banks of ditches near Loch Fada. The root-stock was cut up and steeped in water, and the mucilaginous matter from it applied to sprains.

Botrychium, Sw.

B. lunaria, Sw.—Moonwort. Luan-Lus, C. A few plants on grassy slopes, Creagan.—June. This plant was held in superstitious reverence among Celtic and other nations; horses were said to lose their shoes where it grew. C.

Equisetaceæ (the Horsetail family)

British species are perennial herbs with hollow-jointed stems, marked by longitudinal striæ, without true leaves.

Equisetum, L.

E. arvense, L.—Corn Horsetail. Earball Capuill, I. A common weed of moist fields.

E. sylvaticum, L.—Branched Wood Horsetail. Cuirridín Coille, I. Damp hollow below Allt-ruadh plantation.

E. palustre, L.—Marsh Horsetail. Cuirristín, I. Ditch, roadside, Bealach Gaoithe, and other places.

E. limosum, L.—Smooth Naked Horsetail. Loch side.

E. limosum, b. fluviatile (L).—Ditch below Screadan.

Lycopodiaceæ (the Club-moss family)

Species of the order are widely distributed; but, judging from fossil remains, they were more abundant and grew to a larger size in the earlier geological periods.

Lycopodium, L.

L. Selago, L.—Fir Club-moss. Garbhag-an-t-Sléibh. A few plants among the hills. Perennial. As several were found uprooted, it is possible that the species is being exterminated by grazing stock.

Selaginellaceæ (the Selaginella family)

A large and interesting tropical order, confined in Britain to a few species.

Selaginella, Spring.

S. selaginoides, Gray.—Lesser Alpine Clubmoss. Common in moist situations.—Per.

CELLULAR CRYPTOGAMS

CHARACEÆ (the Stonewort order)

Aquatic perennials with long, slender branching stems, often encrusted with carbonate of lime (hence the name); some species, when handled, emit a vile smell. Fish, especially Carp, are said to thrive best in waters where the different species of Chara abound.

Chara, L.

C. fragilis, Desv.—Cloimh uisge. Common in the lochs and in stagnant peaty water. Said to have the same effect on insects as Keating's powder and to have been similarly used. It has a strong, fetid smell.

C. fragilis, d. barbata, Gant.—Peat-bog pools. Garvard. —May.

C. aspera, Willd.—Deep water, west Loch Fada.—July.

C. contaria, Kuetz.—Kiloran farm, reservoir.

C. vulgaris, L.—Fetid Water Horsetail; Common Stonewort. Machrins shore pools. Confirmed by Rev. G. R. Bullock Webster.

Tolypella, Leonh.

T. glomerata, Leonh.—Shore pools, Machrins.—August. Confirmed by Rev. G. R. Bullock Webster.

Nitella, Agardh.

N. translucens, Agardh.—Loch Sgoltaire.—August.

N. opaca, Agardh.—-West Loch Fada.—July.

APPENDIX

THE islands of the Inner Hebrides are believed to be isolated fragments of what was once a great expanse of land, proof of the former existence of which is found in dizzy sea-cliffs a thousand feet in height, as in the west of Skye, and formed of parallel beds which wind along the coast for miles. Of the enormous waste that has ensued, we have ample evidence in the numerous glens and lochs which have been excavated out of the basaltic masses. The Sound of Mull is, we are told, the work of erosion; and the parallel bars of rocks to be viewed on either side are believed to have been at one time prolonged across the channel.

Of the extent of the great waste that has taken place, much of our present knowledge has been gleaned from that peculiar formation, the Sgùrr of Eigg. It is volcanic in origin, and composed of hard glassy pitchstone resting on the basalt plateau. What is now the crest of a ridge 1289 feet above sea-level—one of the most striking natural objects in the Western Isles, towering hundreds of feet above the highest of the surrounding hills—was, at the time of its formation, according to Sir Archibald Geikie, the bottom of a valley through which flowed a river of sufficient volume to carry boulders of Cambrian sandstone with it from the distant hills of Rum. The hard pitchstone forming the Sgùrr originated from molten lava which poured forth and flowed to the lowest level, where it gradually cooled and hardened. It blocked and filled up the river bed, covering the sandstone, forests of pine, and other debris that in later ages were destined to shed light on the geological history of the islands. The land that once united the basalt plateaux of Eigg to the Cambrian sandstone mountains of Rum, from which drained a large volume of water such as must have flowed along the old river course, has disappeared, and Eigg has become an island. The ascending sides of the valley in which the Sgùrr at one time reposed have been worn away, and are now reduced to slopes which shelve steeply down to the shores. That land, we are told, was one of rich alkali-charged soil; and the buried leaves of Canna and Mull and the pines of Eigg indicate a period of warmer climate than we now enjoy.[1]

[1] Sir A. Geikie's beautiful theory of the Sgùrr of Eigg, given above, has recently been challenged by Mr Harker. It seems likely now that the pitchstone was intruded underground and never reached the surface until laid bare by denudation. It may be noted that this later interpretation makes a greater demand upon erosion than even its predecessor.

INDEX

NATURAL ORDERS AND GENERA OF FLOWERING PLANTS, FERNS, ETC.

GENERAL

(but not including the *general* matter under Orders and Genera)

14

GAELIC NAMES OF PLANTS, BIRDS, ETC.